The Men & Machines
of
Kendall Square

CHARLES RIVER

KENDALL SQUARE

EAST CAMBRIDGE, 1903

The Men & Machines
of
Kendall Square

1880-1930
The Second Industrial Revolution

Sherwood   Stockwell

The Industrial Revolution has two phases: one material, the other social; one concerning the making of things, the other concerning the making of men.

Charles A. Beard

Table of Contents

Kendall Square Landmark Group

Foreword

Kendall Square is a neighborhood in the East Cambridge section of the City of Cambridge, Massachusetts. One could imagine that its draw for innovative people came with the more recent arrival of such famous names as Novartis, Biogen, Pfizer, and Google, but it began long ago. Its status was enhanced with MIT's arrival nearby in 1916, but its reputation as a mecca for inventive men and their machines began in the 1880's and continued through the 1930's. During this half century many things changed: the way we communicated, the way we traveled, the way we ate, the way we lived, where we lived, how we maintained our health, and the way we created machines to do much of the work to make all that possible. At the beginning of those years, the Kendall Square area of Cambridge only held a few industrial structures surrounded by undeveloped open space. What is now Memorial Drive was marshland. Steam and sailing vessels could land bulk goods near the square to be carted off to nearby towns and villages, where the raw materials were fashioned by hand into usable objects or consumable goods. Fabricating an end product only required the exertion of simple human energy. That was true whether making a cake or constructing a brick building.

Invention spurred on by invention would turn Kendall Square into a place where machines manufactured the products that had formerly been made by hand, if at all. The process turned out so much that production began to exceed demand and the producers needed a way to entice consumers. This was a time when words like brand-identity, merchandising, and advertising were invented. In those few years, the single word *manufacture* changed its meaning from *manu facto* to *manu mechanica*. This was also a time when the need for eye-hand coordination would diminish until its major task would be using thumbs to activate a cell-phone.

I first knew Kendall square in the early 1930's, when I accompanied my father on Saturdays to the Barbour Stockwell factory at 205 Broadway. There, while he worked at his desk, I was allowed to visit the pattern shop and envy the carpentry work in the carved wood molds used for castings. If I was lucky, one of the men would take me with him into the foundry next door, where he'd place the molds ready for a Monday pour. In those days, the neighborhood thrived with invention and industry and the operative word was progress. In the previous century, inventors like Benjamin Franklin, Eli Whitney, Elias Howe, and Samuel F. B. Morse had made their homes in the state; and it was a time in Cambridge when other lesser men hoped to challenge existing methods and create new machines that would bring them equal fame. The *Cambridge Chronicle* heralded the city's status in 1905 with:

Cambridge is already a recognized manufacturing center, its factories of a diversified character are prosperous, all are running to the fullest capacity, many of them enlarging their plants, and many new industries have been added in the past year or two.

Alexis de Tocqueville had predicted this zest for American manufacturing in the 1830s.

Americans are constantly driven to engage in commerce and industry. Their origin, their social condition, their political institutions, and even the region they inhabit urge them irresistibly in this direction. Their present condition, then, is that of an almost exclusively manufacturing and commercial association, placed in the midst of a new and boundless continent, which their principal object is to explore for purposes of profit.

De Tocqueville was making his observations near the start of the First Industrial Revolution, whereas the growth of Kendall Square in 1905 coincided with the United State's Second Industrial Revolution. The differences between the two were significant. When it came to inventing new products, in the First Industrial Revolution people only knew *how* things worked; but in the Second Industrial Revolution, thanks to advances in scientific methodology, people began to know *why* things worked. Instead of just knowing that Steam in an engine drove a piston, people began to understand that water when heated expanded into steam and created the energy needed to drive the piston. Armed with increasing sources of scientific knowledge, Inventors began to figure out more ways to supplant human with mechanical action.

To operate a machine that would supplant or replace human action, one needed a source of power. At first, that source was water, so factories were built next to rivers, where waterwheels turned shafts that then could operate a tool like a lathe, With the invention of the steam turbine, however, each factory could create its own power independent of place and the number of machines to utilize that power was only limited by the size of their boilers. Factories grew as bigger boiler plants became available and building the larger facilities required huge sums of money. There were investors who could amass such sums, providing there'd be ample returns. Those returns had to come from manufacturing profits and profits depended upon efficiency. The search for efficiency led to a concentration of workers and machines.Everything got bigger. The economies of scale in the factories were repeated in living quarters that, in turn, increased densities in urban areas where machines and workers could be near gas and water and sewage systems. Concurrently, growing telephone and telegraph networks, expanding railroads, and the ability to distribute electric power over a network of wires vastly increased the areas where products could be sold. Within a few decades, an America once populated with individual farmers dotted across the landscape found many of its citizens bunched together in cities that were rushed into existence without overall plans or realization of the social problems that would result from such a radical change in where and how people work.

View of East Cambridge, 1879

1. Cambridge & Kendall Square

In 1630, dedicated Puritans of the Massachusetts Bay Colony settled on the banks of the Charles River and called their village Newtowne. For a short time, this was the acting capital of the Massachusetts Bay Colony. In 1636, the colony established Harvard, the oldest institution for higher learning in the United States, and it became a magnet for brilliant people like Henry Wadsworth Longfellow and James Russell Lowell. Harvard was located in Old Cambridge, which along with Cambridgeport, and East Cambridge grew within Newtowne's borders until 1846, when the three were combined by charter into the City of Cambridge.

Early Cambridge was accessible from the Charles River, but lacked a harbor where ocean-going ships could load and unload. For that, it depended upon the waterfront city of Boston and meant crossing the Charles by boat. When the West Boston Bridge, now called Longfellow Bridge, was erected in 1793, it reduced the travel distance between the two places from eight to three miles, but still didn't provide Cambridge with its own docking facilities. Atkins Eliot's History of Cambridge described the difficulties of making Cambridge into a major port. "Ambitious plans were made for transforming the riverbank into a commercial port. Docks and canals were dug out of the salt marsh, and, in 1805, Cambridge was made a port of entry. Then came reverses…Of all the docks constructed by the various companies, only Broad canal remains." Broad Canal was in East Cambridge, which otherwise was mostly marsh grasses, mud, and open water. It took an ingenious and sometimes unscrupulous man named Andrew Craigie to raise the money and start the work to turn the land into buildable terrain, with waterfront access to the Charles River. Craigie spent over a dozen years developing East Cambridge after first securing title to large tracts of the land and water; and, more importantly, getting the authority in 1807 from the General Court to build a second bridge between Boston and Cambridge. With the new bridge in place, the New England Glass Company, took over an old warehouse from the defunct Boston Porcelain and Glass Company. Soon, over 1,000 lived in homes on East Cambridge Streets built by glassblowers, laborers, molders, gaffers, and their families. Many of these were immigrants from Europe and displaced French Canadians. Although New England Glass eventually moved out of town, they left East Cambridge with a good supply of the skilled and unskilled labor which would be in place as other industries moved in during the Second Industrial Revolution.

As East Cambridge grew, so did a sub-area known as Kendall Square. Technically the title refers only to the small landscaped plaza left where Broadway meets Main,

Wadsworth, and Third Streets, but overtime the name has become synonymous with much of the neighborhood surrounding the plaza. Factories from the Second Industrial Revolution have been replaced by high-tech industries, and the boundaries of Kendall Square have been pushed out, moving towards the waterfront in one direction and Central Square in the other. At the beginning of the 20th century, one of the first to build in and boost the area was Albert N. Murray whose Murray and Emery Printing Company was located on MainStreet. The story of his company and early Kendall Square was carried in an article of *Our Neighbors at Kendall Square,* which was reprinted in the *Cambridge Tribune* in November, 1923.

> At that time there were many large and old-established industries at Kendall Square, but their number was small compared with that of today. The buildings of the Massachusetts Institute of Technology were then in process of construction. There was no Filene Service Building, no Suffolk Engraving Building, no Arthur D. Little Building, no E. Fleming & Company, no I. L. Hammett Company, no L. E, Knott Apparatus Company, no King-ton Knitting Company, no Manufacturers National Bank. To many, Kendall Square seemed a wilderness for the printing business. We believed the neighborhood had promise of great things --for any business.

In 1915, Albert N. Murray published a monograph to celebrate the opening of the new multi-storied Murray and Emery Printing Company building in Cambridge. Murray's *Story of Kendall Square* described the importance of its ties to Boston:

> The growth of Kendall Square is a story of progress and development…although the history of over a century is so closely entwined about Kendall Square that one is easily carried back to the early days of Boston and Cambridge for a perusal of the history of this locality, now claiming so much attention. Obviously the greatest advantage of Kendall Square is its nearness to the heart of the "hub."
>
> Supplanting the primitive ferry across the Charles River –the natural separation between two cities that otherwise might have been one – by a modest wooden bridge was an advance step, and Kendall square gained a point – or would have if it had been present at the time. The substitution sixty years later, of a more substantial bridge and the introduction of horse cars was another point in favor of Kendall Square.…and then a granite bridge came, and with it the Cambridge Tunnel …(providing a) three-minute ride between Kendall Square and Park Street – and Kendall Square was "made."

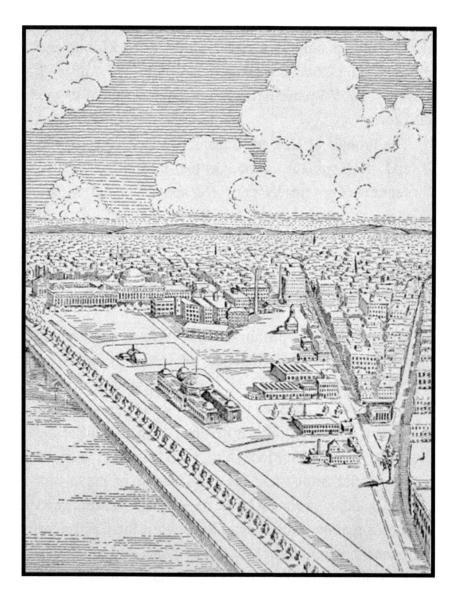

*Sketch of MIT and Kendall Square 1916
from Albert Murray's Book*

Kendall Square was almost not "made." The granite bridge he spoke of, now known as Longfellow Bridge, was constructed with an unfinished heavy rail right-of-way down its center. This was to carry the Cambridge extension of the Boston subway system, the first in the United States and fifth in the world that began construction in 1895 to ease the Hub City's surface traffic. In Boston, carriages and wagons crawled on a maze of narrow, winding streets laid out in some cases along Colonial cow paths. The demand for a new subway was also driven by the Blizzard of 1888, which dumped forty to fifty inches of snow on the city and immobilized trolleys, railroad cars, and every other form of transportation. In 1904, the Cambridge city council asked the state legislature to amend previous acts that authorized an elevated rail line to provide for a subway extending from Harvard Square to Kendall Square. By 1908, the Boston Transit Commission had been created and it proposed construction of the subway; but with only two stations at Harvard Square and Central Square. When Cambridge residents objected, urging a third stop at Kendall Square, the mayor called in prominent transportation engineer William Barclay Parsons, who designed the Cape Cod Canal; and, as chief engineer for the New York IRT, had successfully bored a tunnel for the new subway under New York City. Parson's claimed the Kendall square location was impractical, not only poorly situated but actually dangerous, because of the grade at the approaching streets,

Broadway and Main. Nonetheless, the commissioners finally selected Kendall Square as a station site because they believed that " no scheme of rapid transit for Cambridge is complete without providing for the present and prospective needs of the large and growing manufacturing and residential section of the city through which the subway is to run." The commissioners were right on. Happily, on the first subway ride between Boston and Cambridge, as the conductor called out "Kendall Square", Deacon Edward Kendall was one of the passengers.

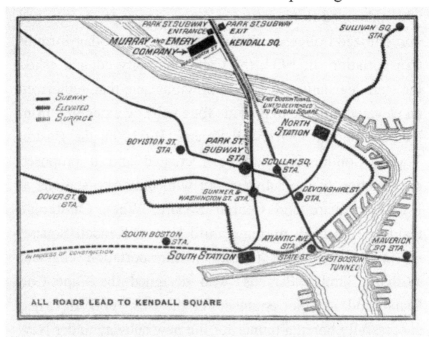

Map of early subway system from Murray's book

Given its designation as a station on the subway system,

Kendall Square was assured its name would survive. Before the turn of the 19th century, it all was separated from the rest of the city by marshy land. As the land was filled and the Broad Canal was dug to connect a system of smaller canals with the main river and the Atlantic Ocean, the Lechmere Point Corporation laid out a rectilinear street grid where lots could be sold off, creating the first planning of its kind in the Boston area. Gradually, buildings were constructed on the lots. In 1816, after Andrew Craigie had closed his deal with Middlesex County, he hired Charles Bulfinch to design the county courthouse and it was erected on 3rd Street. In 1827 the Congregationalists built a Federalist style church based on a design by Asher Benjamin. The New England Glass Company's arrival in 1818 was later followed on Otis and First Streets by A. H. Davenport and Company, a manufacturer of furniture for notable buildings including the White House and a creator of the boxy sofas bearing its name.

In 1869, a charter from the Commonwealth was issued to Gardiner G. Hubbard to establish The East Cambridge Land Co. for the purpose of improving the vacant marsh in East Cambridge lying between Third and Portland streets, Broad, Canal, and Charles streets, and including about three million square feet of land. Laying out and building the streets improved the property, making way for manufacturing industries and mechanical enterprises. Hubbard is credited with being the first to bring the gas company, the waterworks, and the horse railroad to Cambridge; but it was The Grand Junction Railroad and Depot Company that gave the real impetus to industrial development on Hubbard's land in The Point. The railroad branch that ran through the property from north to south offered ready transportation to plants built upon its line and connected them with all the main railroad lines entering Boston from the north and west.

The name Kendall Square first appears in city documents in 1857, memorializing the spot Edward Kendall selected for his Kendall Boiler and Tank Company. Originally a teacher in his hometown of Holden, Massachusetts, Kendall built a factory that is now a national landmark. He extended his property by filling mudflats with material excavated for the extension of the State House on Beacon Hill in Boston. Technically addressed as Deacon Kendall because of his years of service in the Pilgrim Congregational Church, Kendall also served as a four-term Cambridge Alderman, was vice-president of the Cambridge Savings Bank, and was the Prohibition candidate for Governor of the state of Massachusetts in 1895. Although hardly successful as a politician, Edward Kendall and his two sons built a business employing 200 men using 1000 tons of iron and steel a year. One of their larger successes was the construction and installation of a 300 horsepower boiler for the Newton Water Works. In addition to the business successes, his name lives on with the square and its important relationship to the campus of the Massachusetts Institute of Technology.

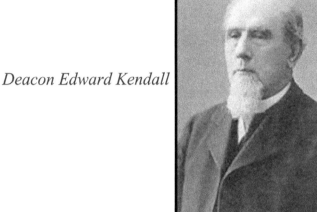

Deacon Edward Kendall

On nearby 3rd Street, Peter Gray built a factory for Peter Gray & Sons in order to manufacture the special signal lights that were critical to operating the red lights that flashed thirty times each minute at railroad crossings, warning the traffic that a train was approaching. Gray also made the first storm-warning lanterns for the U. S. Weather Bureau. During World War I they made aviation field floodlights and flashing signaling lights that were operated by telegraph key. Another type of Gray lantern was known as the "Williams Eye Testing Lantern," created to examine the color perception capabilities of men in the railroad and marine services. The Gray lantern required great accuracy in manufacture and selection of shades of colored glasses.

The headquarters of Benjamin Fox was also located on 3rd street. As a builder, he constructed the Boston Woven Hose Building, where they developed a machine to produce the first rubber-lined multiple-fire hose and also manufactured the *Vim* single tube bicycle tire with a pebble tread. Fox also was the designated architect and engineer for the landmark Hathaway Bakery, where he used the reinforced concrete piles described in a paper he published in the *Journal of the Association of Engineering Societies*, 1909. The object of the paper was "to give a description of the design, construction and data on driving cast reinforced concrete piles for a foundation for the Boston Woven Hose Building." Inasmuch as the first concrete pile was made in France by engineer M. Flennebique in 1896, there was little information on their use and Fox's detailed records of time spent and methods used were an important addition to the body of structural engineering knowledge.

2. Power

Edward Kendall selected East Cambridge because of its low land prices, but he also must have been clairvoyant, realizing that the area would become industrialized and need his boilers to power its machinery. A boiler was basic to the production of steam to power the engines that operated the moving machinery employed in the expanding factories of East Cambridge. The phenomena of using steam to power a primitive engine was first described in the first century AD by Hero of Alexandria. His rotating globe with propulsion jets called an *aeolipile* spun when a water container below was heated.

As early as 1551, Taqi al-Din described a form of steam turbine to be used as a small jack; but Englishman and military engineer Thomas Savery was the first to convert steam energy into usable mechanical energy. In 1698, he invented a means to pump water out of flooded coalmines by condensing steam from a boiler and creating a vacuum that sucked up water from the pits. A few years later, his countryman Thomas Newcomen improved on Savery's idea by using a closed-end cylinder with a piston inside that was moved up and down as the condensing steam formed the vacuum. James Watt improved on the concept in 1769 by introducing steam into each end of the cylinder and making the process double acting. The alternating piston became a force that could be harnessed to drive other machinery; but it was an American inventor named Oliver Evans who designed the first high-pressure, non-condensing engine in 1804. His system used the steam itself to provide the power, rather than condensing it to create a vacuum. James Watt improved on Evan's idea, using steam to pump bellows for blast furnaces, to power huge hammers for shaping and strengthening forged metals, and to turn machinery at textile mills. As the concept advanced, it was adapted to operate saws, and by 1829 to propel powerboats and railways. Almost half a century later, the first steam-powered automobiles were invented. One, the Doble, was built by Abner Doble, an MIT alumnus that developed the Model E with his three brother. Although there were more than 60,000 steam cars produced in the United States between 1897 and 1927, the steam engine eventually gave way to gasoline fired engines.

The History of Middlesex County, published in 1880, described the many industries in Cambridge that used steam power to operate machinery. In a newly constructed four-story building on Broadway, the *Thayer Chemist* basement held "the engine and 'drug mill' – the latter fitted with the requisite machinery for grinding and powdering all the articles used." *F. H. Holton* on Harvard Street in Cambridgeport employed a 350 horsepower engine to assist "260 men and boys" in rolling sheet metal to use as roofing and manufacture copper bathtubs. Holton described the latter as a "remunerative" product. The *Cambridge Rolling Mill* required similar steam power to create wrought iron from imported Swedish iron and scrap iron. Their 140 day and nighttime employees were paid between $1.50 and $6.00 per day depending upon their skills. At the *Riverside Press,* one of three publishing houses in Cambridge, 600 male and female employees depended upon a magnificent 100 horsepower *Corliss* engine to operate all of the machinery used in their four-story building on the banks of the Charles River.

Wiped out by successive fires in 1857 and 1873, The *George G. Page Box Company* finally built brick buildings to produce their boxes and packing cases. On the outside of Factory No. 1, a brick boiler and engine house contained boilers with capacities of 150 and a 125 horsepower. *George W. Gale*, then the largest lumber dealer in Cambridge, required a Campbell boiler, not just to power an engine, but to keep stored lumber at a constant temperature of 70 degrees. Steam pipes running through his storage shed thoroughly seasoned every board, in his words "making them superior to kiln-dried lumber."

first, families like the Sands made bricks by hand, digging out the clays with picks and shovels; and, after mixing the batch, throwing the molded shapes into a kiln. Typically, the clays sat near the surface, but as the clay pits were dug deeper they hit ground water; so George Blake, a mechanical engineer, invented an innovative pump using steam to keep brickyards free of water. The firm of Blake & Knowles Steam Pump Works began in 1864 when Blake and two partners, brickyard owners Peter Hubbell and Job A. Turner, started to manufacture pumps in Boston. In 1889 the company returned to Cambridge and built a building, a machine shop and office at 265 Third Street. The company employed 1,000 workers by 1896 and manufactured a wide range of pumps for a variety of industrial applications, finally merging Blake & Knowles and seven affiliated companies to become the Worthington Pump & Machinery Corporation in 1916. Their original building has been designated a national landmark.

At the start, *Kennedy's Bakery* on Main Street could only bake four barrels of flour daily to turn out crackers "rolled and docked singly by hand." After introducing steam power, Artemas Kennedy increased his production to nine barrels of flour per day. This meant that each day the bakery devoured 6000 eggs, 1400 pounds of butter, 3400 pounds of lard, 170 gallons of milk, 150 gallons of molasses, two tons of sugar, and smaller amounts of raspberry jam, raisins, currants, and spices. Their sugar came from the nearby *Revere Sugar Refinery* who produced about 1200 barrels of sugar per day in a six-story building on Water Street.

The city was bustling. In North Cambridge, where potters originally worked by hand, *A. H. Hew & Co.* introduced steam-powered machinery to operate the wheels used to produce *Earthen-Ware* flower pots and to ornament *Albertine* vases made from local clays. Soap manufacturers installed steam-powered equipment, expanding their supply sources by importing alkali from England, borax from California, perfume from China, Germany, or France. In the 1830's these materials could be unloaded and the finish product exported using local docks.   More soap was shipped from Cambridge than any other United States port to such places as the West Indies and South America. The ships carrying as many as 5,000 boxes of soap to the South returned with cargoes of coffee and gold. By 1880, overseas shipments had almost ceased, but there were still five large soap factories in Cambridge making "many million pounds per annum."

In the late 1800's, power in Cambridge factories was additionally upgraded with the use of gas for heating and illumination. The gas was created by passing high-pressure steam over hot coal. The reaction produced a mixture of carbon dioxide and hydrogen that was cooled and scrubbed to produce hydrogen gas that was delivered via a 127-mile network of pipes reaching all over the city. The Cambridge Gas Light Co. on Third Street had one of the largest plants in the state. It included three immense gas holders, the largest a landmark 210-foot diameter cylinder that rose up and down within a 165-foot high steel cage.

The operation of machinery within these plants depended upon steam power, created by burning coal that had to be delivered to the site. Almost every factory had its own tall, brick chimney to evacuate the resulting smoke and fumes. As new ways to manufacture were discovered, so were sources of fuel: manufacturers in major cities could obtain natural gas by the 1820's and petroleum after it was discovered in Titusville, Pennsylvania in 1859. New energy sources prompted new ways to use them and made new avenues for inventors to follow. The goal was always towards exchanging mechanical for muscle power and shortening the time it took to turn out a finished product.

At the turn of the 19th century, industries in East Cambridge were continually looking for advanced ways to power their equipment. Most of it had been running for years on elaborate systems of drive shafts turned by a complicated collection of belts whirring from overhead shafts that were in turn powered from a central steam turbine and boiler plant. The Kendall Square manufacturers were eager and ready for power from electricity. First, however, they needed an easy and efficient system to transmit the new power source, and there were conflicting ways to do this. In 1879, when Thomas Edison invented the light bulb, it was powered by a direct current. For years, Edison championed this as the best way to distribute electricity. It could be generated from a central source, and by 1887 there were 121 Edison power stations serving customers scattered across the United States. Actually, all these stations only served a few customers, because direct current (DC) could only be sent along wires for a distance of a mile before its power diminished. Things changed when Nikola Tesla discovered that an alternating current (AC) could be sent long distances over relatively small wires at a conveniently high voltage. The voltage could be reduced as needed by individual customers. Alternating-current generating stations could be larger, more efficient, and the distribution wires were relatively less costly. It took time, however, to make a general switch to AC current because of a bitter rivalry between Thomas Edison and Nikola Tesla. Edison insisted that Tesla's alternating current was too dangerous and he publicly electrocuted animals with Tesla's AC current to prove his point. The early victims were dogs and cats, but the most dramatic display came when Edison supposedly electrocuted an elephant named *Topsy*. *Wired* magazine ran a story with the headline "Edison Fries an Elephant to Prove His Point." Actually, the animal had been sentenced to death by Luna Park officials after she had killed three handlers during the previous three months.

The first DC was supplied from stations owned by Edison Electric, which later became General Electric; but in 1886 George Westinghouse began building Tesla's AC system. After Westinghouse's company won the bid to supply electricity to the 1893 World's Columbian Exposition in Chicago, most suppliers switched to AC. By 1905, the Cambridge Electric Light Company had a plant with a 255-foot high chimney belching smoke from burning coal that produced steam to drive turbines producing the electricity. This AC electricity could be transmitted over wires to any manufacturer in the city. One thing that made that easier was the invention of insulated wire that separated positive from negative lines. This was conceived and produced by Simplex Wire & Cable in Kendall Square, which also produced one of the first underwater cables. After momentous years building and expanding, Cambridge was truly contributing to the material gains of the Second Industrial Revolution.

.128"/.460" TELEPHONE CABLE

3. Iron Founder

For the most part, the need for power in Kendall Square and East Cambridge lay with companies making disposable consumer goods like soap, breadstuff, and sweets. These companies benefited from the new sources of power that operated the ever-improving machines of the Second Industrial Revolution, replacing tedious human labor and in turn reducing the costs of production and the ultimate price of the product. Manufacturers were also adapting Henry Ford's idea of an assembly line to their own production; and often the creation of one type of machine led to the invention of other machines. Although some *machine tools*, that is machines that helped people make things, were created in-house, the Kendall Square area had its own machine tool manufacturer, a young organization that would soon fill the gore created by the intersection of Broadway and Hampshire Street.

Walworth Barbour would become a co-founder of the new firm. He was born in Saratoga Springs, New York, on Christmas Day, 1850. As a boy, Walworth was exposed to a genteel society and family heritage that would help his future pursuits. He watched the town grow after the Saratoga and Schenectady Railroad extended its tracks to Saratoga Springs, eager to draw passengers to the unique mineral waters that flowed from the earth with carbon dioxide in solution. Health enthusiasts would have had to go all the way to Colorado to find a similar source of catharsis. Large resort hotels, built to house the spa devotees, also welcomed sportsmen and bettors in 1863 to the grand opening of the Saratoga Race Course.

The Walworth name first appeared in Saratoga Springs in 1832 when Chancellor Reuben Hyde Walworth purchased the simple colonial house on Broadway known as Pine Grove. The Walworth family roots were dug deep enough to rise above those merely seeking the cures of carbonized water and the excitement of the track. Their social status, however, was somewhat tarnished by the plight of Ellen Hardin, who married Mansfield Tracy Walworth in 1852, only to find him unstable and a wife-beater. Despite her obtaining a "limited divorce," Mansfield continued threats and physical assaults against Ellen until their son Frank couldn't tolerate his father's actions and shot him to death. The episode was scandal enough to rate its documentation in a book by Geoffrey O'Brien entitled *The Fall of the House of Walworth* .

Walworth Barbour spent his early years working as a civil engineer in the Adirondacks. Moving to Cambridge in 1874, he worked as a clerk for the Walworth Manufacturing Company at 368 Main Street. The company was an outgrowth of a New York firm that was created in 1842 by ancestor, James Jones (JJ) Walworth. JJ moved the company to Boston and began to produce radiators and other elements that operated a central heating and ventilation system he'd developed for hotels, theatres, and churches. JJ and his brother Caleb, a purported mechanical genius and inventor, also produced generators to provide gas lighting in large buildings and developed a line of valves to control the flow of steam, water, and gas. Their most lasting product, however, was the *Stillson Wrench* that was invented by an employee named Dan Stillson. When Walworth Barbour joined what had become Walworth Manufacturing, the company was one of the first to pioneer an 8-hour workday, hire women as secretaries when such was uncommon, and provide them with those new machines called typewriters. It was also the place where, in 1878, Alexander Graham Bell used the company's telegraph connection between the Cambridge and Boston offices to demonstrate the first "long-distance" telephone call. In 1882, the building housing the Walworth Manufacturing Company on Main Street was torn down and the Walworth company moved to South Boston to a new two-story brick building, which contained Morrell & Allen, manufacturers of steam engines, William Campbell & Co., makers of locomotive and marine boilers; and *Walworth O. Barbour & Co.,* machinists employing 40 men.

Formerly listed as a clerk at Walworth Manufacturing, Walworth Barbour was designated an *iron founder* in the Cambridge Directories running from 1882 to

1889. Simpson Bolland described what that meant in *THE IRON FOUNDER SUPPLEMENT of 1893.*

> It is the business of the iron founder to produce castings which will best meet all of the numerous demands – fineness combined with hardness, fineness combined with softness, strength to resist pressures and strains, etc. He must be able, by a judicious selection of different brands of iron, to produce mixtures that will meet the almost impossible demands created by faults in construction as well as the countless conditions, which, owing to the nature of the case, are imperative, and can only be met successfully by correct mixtures.

Casting had its eccentric demands, which were encountered first in the 4th century BC, when a Chinaman poured molten metal into a mold that matched the final dimensions of a finished part. The art was carried on and, as demand increased for more complex assemblies during the Second Industrial Revolution, castings were needed when cutting, hammering, or bending a simple metal shape couldn't produce the desired result. Iron founders had been easily making things like piping elbows and sewer grates; but they became more important as inventors devised machines that needed parts that had never been made before. An iron founder's work depended upon skilled woodworkers, who first sculpted a mock-up or pattern of the needed part. This was set within a box of sand to make a mold, into which molten metal was poured. As Bolland cautioned, the whole process could fail if the mix of the metal was wrong and the casting cracked as it cured. An experienced iron monger could usually avoid such lure. Today the process also involves a knowledge of chemistry and metallurgy and has the advantage of advanced technical gauges, measuring devices, and robot-operated handling equipment. In Walworth Barbour's time, however, there was only his own knowledge and acumen to minimize throwbacks and the mettle of the thirty-year old owner who was supervising the operation was continually tested.

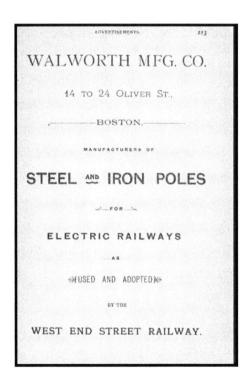

4. Machinist

Fred F. Stockwell, Jr. was born a dozen years after Walworth Barbour, in the town of Brattleboro, Vermont that was about ninety miles east of Saratoga Springs. There were similarities in the two birthplaces. Both towns were former hunting grounds for Native Americans: the Mohawks in Saratoga Springs and the Abenakis in Brattleboro. Both towns were located on rivers: Saratoga Springs on the Hudson and Brattleboro on the Connecticut. Both towns had tourist-attracting spring waters, although the social niceties of bathing in the carbonized water of Saratoga Springs could hardly compare with the *Brattleboro Water Cure* championed by Dr. Robert Wesselhoeft and described in the *New Haven Courier.*

The tormentor first spreads a blanket, and then over it a thick sheet just wet in water of 46 deg. Fahrenheit. Upon this the shivering patient extends his length, and feels himself enveloped in its heart chilling folds. "But that is nothing." Before him is the terrible plunge bath...One splash, and he rises to the top feeling an icicle thrust in his heart. Then a dry rubbing with a sheet...and he struts forth to meet the sun, with nerves braced up to a pitch that he cares not what he meets.

Water Cure Polka,
Christian Schuster,
Dedicated To
Dr. Robert Wesselhoeft.

This icy approach to life in Fred Stockwell's birthplace versus the warming comfort of Walworth Barbour's home might have modestly shaped their respective personalities. There were more secular differences, however, between the Saratoga Springs of Walworth Barbour's childhood and Fred Stockwell's Brattleboro. The name Walworth was an old and venerable one in New York State. Chancellor Reuben Hyde Walworth was appointed to its highest judicial office and subsequently brought the name and his fame to Saratoga Springs, where he established the estate that became a residence for generations of Walworths that followed him. The name Stockwell came to the Brattleboro area in the 1860's when Abel Stockwell became the first settler in the adjacent town of Marlborough. One of his Brattleboro relatives was a tobacco farmer and another owned a tavern on Ames Hill; but Abel's most notable ancestor was his grandfather Quinton Stockwell, who was captured by Indians in 1677, escaped death burning at the stake, was force-marched in rain and snows to Canada as a prisoner of the French; and, after being set free a year later, he was miraculously able to dictate a long report on his captivity.

Census records show that both Fred F. Stockwell Jr. and his father left Vermont and were living in Belmont, Massachusetts in 1865. Fred F. Jr. was then three years old. They were not the only ones to leave town. A 2015 study showed, "in each decade between 1850 and 1900, about 40 percent of native-born Vermonters left the state." There were plenty of reasons for that. Settlers that had been drawn north to the alluvial soils along the Connecticut river soon learned that dirt farming in Vermont was fraught with weather problems. The Civil War hurt others with ties to cotton and the *Triangle Trade*, whose incomes were so diminished they were forced to move away. The Stockwell move may have also been an economic necessity. Fred Junior's grandfather was one of the many in the state forced into bankruptcy in the long recession of 1839-1843. He may have had to sell the family lands, leaving nothing to pass on to the son. Add to that the hellish winter 0f 1861-62, whose twenty-seven snowstorms totaling a depth of nine feet, six inches could have sapped both strength and savings. A   story passed down through generations told how young Fred found a job as a stable boy. On one lucky day the usual driver for a wealthy man named Walworth O. Barbour was sick and Fred was given the job. From the first, the twelve year's older Barbour was impressed with

Fred, who then became the permanent driver for Barbour. On one of these journeys Walworth asked about Fred's future. "A bright young man like you must want to do something with your life besides drive a hack?" To this, Fred said he wanted to become a machinist, whereupon Barbour paid for his initial training.

By 1880, Fred was listed in the census as an apprentice machinist, aged 17. Records show that he worked for eight years for the W. O. Taylor Company that specialized in making machines that turned out crackers. During those eight years as apprentice and then machinist, Fred became an expert using machine tools to produce metal parts that conformed to a set of specifications, or tolerances, typically defined in a set of engineering drawings. He would have had to learn how to read those drawings or blueprints and develop a knowledge of engineering lingo used on the documents. Finally, he needed to master the tools required to do the work of cutting, boring, grinding, and shearing metals. By 1886, Fred was well qualified to start his own machine shop.

5. Machine Tools

Historians say the first machine tool was a lathe developed around 1438 to produce screw threads out of wood. By 1840, machinists were using tools like the slide rest lathe, screw-cutting lathe, turret lathe, milling machine, pattern tracing lathe, shaper, and metal planer, all accurate enough to produce interchangeable parts. In practice, a machinist typically fabricated similar screw threads for a given product; and one would have to recut new screws if they were trying to make repairs. The problem of interchangeability was solved in England when Henry Maudslay designed and built a screw-cutting engine lathe that repeatedly cut accurate screw threads and allowed the industry to standardize the size and pitch of nuts and bolts. That's also where John Wilkinson invented an accurate boring machine and James Nasmyth invented the shaper.

The machine tool industry was growing in East Cambridge. The Blanchard Machine Company was located at 64 State Street, near what is now the MIT campus. It made machines to produce fertilizer and soap powder. Their new 20,000 square foot two-story building replaced a former Boston location that had been destroyed by fire. At 121 First Street, Seelye Manufacturing Company, successor to the Hawkins Machine Company that had been in Cambridge since 1873, had 15,000 square feet of floor space where they produced machines to make W. L.

Douglas and Regal shoes. As opposed to a strong-handed shoemaker pushing each thread through leather, Seelye machines did all the work. Both Blanchard and Seelye depended upon the services of outside pattern makers like Dixon and Fallis at Main and Osborne Street that made models and the molds used in iron foundries. They also needed accurate toolmakers to finish the process. Now head of his own firm of Walworth Barbour & Co, Walworth Barbour could see the advantages of putting all those Seelye operations under one roof. His foundry could produce multiple shapes where tolerances for their dimensions were not critical. To produce more complicated parts, however, Walworth added pattern makers and machinists to produce not just singular cast iron parts but complete tools to manufacture the consumer goods - candy, soap, biscuits, and bread – all produced by a number of neighboring factories in a burgeoning Cambridge.

By 1886,Walworth had spent eighteen years in the greater Boston area and with his Saratoga Springs heritage and time spent as clerk and paymaster for Walworth Manufacturing, he met people easily and had a good knowledge of Cambridge industry. He would have learned that the business of W.O. Taylor, Fred Stockwell's employer, that had been in operation since 1825, was losing its position as a leading machine tool maker. At this point, Walworth O. Barbour and Fred Stockwell were in a position to join forces. There are no official records of how the two agreed to go into partnership, but its highly possible that Walworth, already with an active foundry business and definitely the senior of the two, decided to acquire Taylor when business was at a low ebb; and, as an added dividend, Fred came along as part of the acquisition.

This was a time when mergers and acquisitions were readily acceptable words in the business world. Nationally, Andrew Carnegie was still buying up smaller companies to create what would become the United States Steel Company and John D. Rockefeller was merging oil producers and distributors to create the Standard Oil Company. This was before Teddy Roosevelt began "busting the trusts," and a time when putting together small, often losing companies in order to make one efficient and profitable entity made great sense, especially to the ones who arrived on top. The idea wasn't lost in East Cambridge. In 1889, Walworth and Fred bought out Alfred Morrell & Co. that had started out in 1858 as Davenport & Bridges, car builders. The name changed to Allen & Endicott, changed again to Morrell & Allen; and finally changed to Alfred Morrell & Co. John P. Winlock, who had been in charge of Morrell's foundry, and H.R. Luther, a Morrell inventor, joined Walworth and Fred as partners in a new Barbour, Stockwell & Co. In 1890, that company was incorporated under Massachusetts' laws with a paid-up capital of $100,000.

On March 19,1892, a column of the *Cambridge*

Chronicle described Barbour Stockwell & Co. as a *Progressive Young Cambridge Firm* and a headline highlighted its *Origin and Accomplishments in Six Years.* It told that they produced seven bakery ovens for the N.Y. Biscuit Company, twenty machines for braiding picture cord wire and a machine for hoisting hogs out of the scalding vats for the North Packing and Provision Company. The *Chronicle* article detailed how Mr. Barbour had charge of the bookkeeping and finances, Mr. Winlock was in charge of the foundry, Mr. Luther was on the road, and Mr. Stockwell had responsibility for the machine shop and remaining departments. It ended with this: "No concern has a cleaner or better reputation than this.It is a credit to the city. Long may it live and prosper."

Barbour was probably the impetus for a number of additional mergers and acquisitions. The company secured the rights to produce something called the Goetz patented box anchor and post cap. These metal parts securely attached wood posts and beams to masonry walls, and were widely used in constructing the large mill-framed, brick buildings that were springing up along New England rivers, using water to power new industries like textiles and shoe making. Then came the acquisition of Denio & Roberts, founded in Boston about 1850, that made the first machines for cutting crackers and biscuits from a sheet of dough. For a long time, their machines were the only ones on the market or in general use to manufacture baked goods. The addition of Denio & Roberts added a new line of products that the company was quick to announce with newspaper ads.

BARBOUR-STOCKWELL CO.
General Machinists and Iron Founders

Street Railway Special Work   Machinery Castings

BAKERS' AND CONFECTIONERS' MACHINERY

205 BROADWAY,   CAMBRIDGE

One of those Denio & Roberts machines was a *Rayne's Patent Reel Oven*, where the revolving reel moved breads in and out of an oven. Having such a patent, however, only assured the firm of a temporary market. In an era of innovation there was always the chance for someone else to expand on an idea, as Arthur Gilman explained in *The Cambridge of Eighteen Hundred and Ninety-six.*

As the manufacturers of bakery products began to educate the public taste by supplying a better quality and a far greater variety of goods, their business increased very rapidly, and the old machines were not accurate enough, nor of sufficient capacity to meet the increased demand. This led to many improvements...Today there is little, and in most bakeries, no hand work done.

Walworth Barbour, only fifty years old, died in 1901. Fred Stockwell took over the presidency and the name was modified to Barbour Stockwell Company. Fred continued to acquire other companies, apparently creating enterprises too small to fall under the rules of the 1890 Sherman Anti-Trust Act. In 1928, he bought out the Broadway Iron Foundry and the Blanchard Instrument Company, and in 1929, the Beaudry Company, a manufacturer of power hammers that shaped metal parts. In 1930, S.J. Clarke Publishing Co. published this in *The History of Massachusetts Industry* by Orra L. Stone: "As the result of consolidations of several distinct business enterprises the Barbour Stockwell Company is now constituted as to be the only concern of its type in New England, viewed from the point of diversification of manufacturers."

Luther, Winlock, and Fred continued as partners in Barbour Stockwell. From the start they had the vision to add machinist's skills to the iron founder to provide straight line solutions for machines that could produce goods. They looked for customers making consumer items like candy, biscuits, bread, and soap. They also looked for places where parts would wear out, as in street railways where damaged switches and connectors needed quick replacement. Their catalog of baking machinery included patented ovens, mixers, beaters, rolling machines, cutting machines, brakes, scrapping and panning machines, peel machines, and cake and biscuit cutters of all kinds. The company outgrew the old Morrell facilities at

356 Main Street in Cambridge. They selected a new two-acre site for a factory in the gore created by the intersection of Broadway and Hampshire Street, with the official address of 205 Broadway. There they built a 175 by 75-feet foundry, a wareroom and pattern storage building, and a three-story building to house the machine shop: a total floor area of 38,300 square feet.

As the business expanded into a permanent home, it also attempted to reward its workers. In 1893 Barbour Stockwell abolished the "piece" system of employee payment and they reduced the working day for foundrymen from ten hours a day to nine, but didn't reduce their take-home pay. They were tougher two years later, however, when the Iron Molders Union tried to get them to settle pay and working grievances. Instead of receiving higher wages, the union members were summarily locked out. It happened again in 1897. Not for long, however, because the company needed to get the men back to work producing parts for an expanding Cambridge Railroad. This, the first street railway in Metropolitan Boston started as a line to link Harvard Square with Boston's West End. It expanded to serve over four miles of track in Somerville near Fred's new home. Most of the rail cars were horse-driven and as the lines grew they needed switches to shift from one line to another. Barbour Stockwell made those switches and, where two lines crossed, they manufactured the grooved plates known as frogs that were used to shift directions.

The parts for machines to produce goods or railways to carry people were either milled from solid bars using what now seem like primitive lathes or they were cast in a foundry and then finished off by machinists. The Barbour Stockwell foundry could both machine solid steel and produce castings of anything that could be made by pouring molten metal into a form. Their large market included cities and towns that needed man-hole frames, covers and grates, catch basin covers and traps, gutter frames and grates for driveways and foot paths, and miscellaneous sewer castings of many kinds. To produce this wide range of products, the company had experienced men like John Winlock, who ran the foundry and H.R. Luther, who held a patent on the Luther Grate.

To produce an item in the foundry, expert woodworkers had to first build up and carve out wood patterns that duplicated the things to be cast and those patterns were then used to shape sand molds. On a given day of the week, the foundry fires were heated up to a melting point and the metal made liquid by the fires was dropped into the molds. If the resulting part was too rough it could be modified in the machine shop. If the required part was better milled than cast, a machinist could fabricate it with metal-working lathes and drills. The machinery to do this was driven by a bewildering complex of wide leather belts that hung down from revolving cylinders above that in turn were powered by a separate steam boiler.

Electricity to replace the noisy and awesome pattern of belts, shafts and wheels hadn't yet arrived on Broadway.

Barbour Stockwell 205 Broadway, Cambridge 1920

In November 1894, The *Cambridge Chronicle* reported that "Business was good, much larger than last year" at Barbour Stockwell & Co. In December 1897, the newspaper told a different story. It was about Thomas H. Snow, a pitiable wreck of his former self, now behind bars in Station 2 in Cambridge. His once portly form had whittled down to 140 pounds. This man, whose white hair and mustache, ruddy complexion, and fine bearing had always hid his 65 years to a considerable degree, was noted for clothing of the latest cut and his extremely neat appearance. Gaunt and ill-fed, Snow's white hands that had never before known what hard toil meant were now scratched and dirty. His coat that usually was arranged with great care, was held together with safety pins. Snow had been attempting to sneak back to his home, having tramped most of the way on railroad tracks and through swamps from Chicago, after running out of the $5,000 he'd embezzled over a five year period from men who had trusted him and looked upon him as a friend: the owners of Barbour Stockwell Company.

In 1930, S.J. Clarke Publishing Co. published *The History of Massachusetts Industry* by Orra L. Stone that summarized the abilities of the Barbour Stockwell Company.

The present organization is divided into eight distinct departments; and in building on one of its principal slogans, "From your ideas to the finished product," the Barbour Stockwell Company through its engineering and production departments is able to seize an idea or principle, translate it to a blue-print, and carry it through its mechanical evolutions, via the wood or metal pattern route to its own foundry for moulding, casting and rough finishing in grey iron, semi-steel, brass, bronze, aluminum, or special alloy, and onto the finishing and fitting in the machine department where all parts can be assembled and where the original idea takes a tangible form in a machine that functions efficiently. Following tests and such changes as are considered necessary, the completed machine can be knocked down, shipped, delivered, installed and started on the peculiar mission it was designed for.

The executives of the Barbour Stockwell Company have ever been cognizant that they were living and acting in an era of engineering advancement; and they early saw that the development of the aircraft industry now in its infancy, was bound to demand better and faster engines and more advanced machinery for the production of power units, instruments, and accessories. They planned accordingly and today their engineering and research, pattern, foundry, machine, power hammer, instrument, and forging and heat treating departments are striving to keep up with the demands made upon them for products, a market now so heavy as to extend beyond the highest point of production reached by the concern even during the period of the World War.

1916 Area Map

6. Candy

In a real sense, Kendall Square was an exceedingly sweet spot fifty years ago. Main Street was affectionately called Confectioner's Row, and the companies along the Row and around the Square made products that are still known and loved today. Mouthwatering brands included the Fig Newton made by the Kennedy Biscuit Factory, Necco Wafers from the New England Confectionery Company, Nut Zippers by Squirrel Brands, Hard Candies from the George Close Company, Daggett Chocolates, the Charleston Chew from the Fox Cross Company, and Junior Mints, Sugar Daddies, **Sugar Mamas and** Sugar Babies from James O. Welch. Today, conglomerates like Nabisco produce the Fig Newton, the oldest survivor Necco makes Daggett Chocolates and Tootsie Roll Industries turns out the Charleston Chew as well as many of the Welch labels.

Oliver Chase making wafers

Candy history goes back as far as 1500 BC, when ancient Egyptians made a confectionery by mixing honey with figs, nuts, and dates. Native Americans invented sugar candy around 250 BC; and the first packaged chocolate candy appeared in England as Whiteman's Chocolate in 1854. In colonized America, pharmacists, that pressed prescription drugs into a sugared lozenge that the patient could suck, began to use the same process to make enjoyable sweets. Towards the end of the 19th century, the ability to produce individual sweets in quantity created North American candies like Wrigley's Juicy Fruit Chewing Gum, Leo Hirshfield's Tootsie Rolls, Necco Wafers, and Hershey's milk chocolate bar. The industry that later brought many more confection makers to Cambridge began in 1765 when Irishman John Hannon built America's first chocolate factory, using water from the Neponset River in Dorchester to power his mill. Sailing ships brought Hannon the cocoa beans from Central America that were vital to making his chocolate. They also carried cane from the Caribbean islands to be processed at the Revere Sugar Company near Miller's River in East Cambridge. Successful candy makers in Boston soon outgrew their locations and moved to cheaper lands in Cambridge, which was mostly open space except for the small enclave of Harvard University. In its favor, Cambridge also had easy access to boats using the Charles River. Fred L. Daggett was one of those who started in

Boston in 1892 and moved Daggett Chocolates to Cambridge in 1925, where he produced more than 40 brands in a factory covering an entire city block. It made little difference whether you purchased *Daggett's Chocolates, Page and Shaw, Lowney's, Apollo, Gobelin, Handspun, Old Homestead* or some 30 other name chocolates. They were all owned by Fred L. Daggett.

John Hannon imported *Cacao* beans from Guatemala, where Maya and Aztecs had been fermenting the sweet fruit of the chocolate tree to make a 5% alcoholic beverage as early as 1900 BC. They called it the "food of the gods." The beans from the fruit were fermented and then roasted to remove the shells. The remaining ingredients were ground to produce a chocolate liquor which in turn broke down into *cocoa* solids and *cocoa* butter. The relative sweetness of a chocolate product depended upon the amount of solids, butter, and sugar in the mix. The kind of chocolate produced by Hannon took on a new form with the advent of *Milk Chocolate*, which had a softer, less snappy texture than the dark variety.

*Ad from
Peter's Chocolates*

A Swiss named Daniel Peter was the first to make that Milk Chocolate, getting the idea from his friend Henry Nestle, who had developed a process that added what was called a "milky flour" into baby food. The challenge for Peter was to find a similar way to produce a stable chocolate product that would not quickly deteriorate and become rancid. After many trials and errors, he achieved success by extracting as much moisture as possible from the mixture. Forming what became the Swiss Chocolate Company to manufacture it, Peter eventually produced his milk chocolate bar under the Nestle label. The new kind of candy became an American confection after caramel maker Milton Hershey discovered Nestle's milk chocolate at the Chicago World's Fair in 1893. He quickly switched his production to chocolate and started to turn out the ubiquitous *Hershey Bar*. The market was broadened in World War I when the US Army distributed the new confection to the troops, commending it as high-calorie soldier's rations.

The Necco Company building with its wafer striped water tower is still a major fixture in the Kendall Square corridor, even though the company moved out in 2003. The Necco wafer is the oldest, continually manufactured candy item in the United States. It got its start in 1847 when an English druggist named Oliver R. Chase, founded Chase and Company, with his brother Silas. They had been pressing prescription drugs into lozenges by hand until Oliver invented a machine to simplify the process. He also invented and patented a machine to pulverize sugar, making it easier to add sweetener to any confection. His pharmacy-inspired machine soon began turning out candies and Chase was one of twenty candy makers exhibiting their machines, most powered by steam, at the 1876 Centennial Exposition in Philadelphia. The candies from Chase's machines were first called "Hub Wafers" because they were manufactured in Boston, dubbed by Oliver Wendell Holmes as the *Hub of the Solar System*. While Chase was turning out his lozenges, the firm of Wright and Moody was spreading sugared joy with children's packages of gumdrops and other novelties; and confectioner Daniel Fobes was patenting a mixture of coffee and cacao called *Mocha*. While Americans were enjoying singular sugar wafers, hard candy, and chocolate bars, in Paris, France, they invented the *enrober,* a machine that could automatically apply coating to a molded fondant, making it possible to combine the individual elements and produce chocolate-covered candy at much lower costs. Enter the *Milky Way,* made by Frank Mars in Minneapolis and the *Mars Bar* made in England by Frank Mars' son, Forrest Mars.

A Shakespearean actor named Donley Cross began making candy in the 1900's after a back injury forced him off the stage. He joined Charlie Fox in 1920 to open the Fox-Cross Company, whose plant at 26 Landsdowne Street near the Necco factory produced a vanilla flavored nougat bar called the *Charleston Chew,* capitalizing on the popular dance of the day. An *enrober* covered the bar with chocolate. At 243 Broadway in Cambridge, George Close, who started his candy company in 1879, produced chocolates, suckers, lemon drops and butter balls. He was better known, however, for a unique advertising program that he'd borrowed from the tobacco companies. In 1911, the Close company began to offer a thirty card set of baseball cards with names like Cy young and Ty Cobb overprinted with slogans like "Home Run! For Close's Butter Balls" and "You're Safe! If You Eat Close's Chocolates." The idea was picked up in 1934 by **the Goudey Gum company of Boston. On the most popular cards ever produced, there were picture s of all the era's stars, including Babe Ruth, Lou Gehrig and Jimmie Foxx.**

In 1901,Oliver Chase merged his operation with Hayward & Company, which had previously absorbed confectioners Ball & Fobes, and Wright & Moody, a confectionery company based in Boston and founded in 1856. This triple merger created the New England Confectionary Company, which in turn manufactured the wafers now carrying the acronym *Necco*. Necco Wafers were so popular that explorer Donald MacMillan took them along in 1913 for nutrition and as "rewards to Eskimo children." An important competitor that Necco eventually acquired, the D. L. Clark Company, started up in 1906 making candy and *Teaberry* gum in Pittsburgh. It's founder David Clark was born in Ireland and came to America when he was eight years old. He started in the candy business working as a salesman in New York, then moved to Pittsburgh to make candy in two back rooms of a small house, and sold his candy from a wagon on neighborhood streets. In 1917, D. L. Clark produced the *Clark Bar* and shipped it overseas to Yankee soldiers fighting in Europe. The cost: five cents. By 1920, Clark was making about 150 different types of candy. Another competitor, the Charles N. Miller Company made a sticky combination of molasses and peanut butter called a *Mary Jane*. The name's source was probably the popular comic strip character, but Miller, eager to avoid any copyright lawsuits, claimed the candy was named after his aunt. The candy's name was not as important to some historians as the fact that the bar was first sold out of what had been Paul Revere's home. Today, Mary Janes are manufactured by Necco.

The New England Confectionery Company continued its dominance of the candy-manufacturing business through much of the first half of the 20th century. During World War II the U.S. Government requisitioned a major portion of the production of *Necco* wafers, because the candy didn't melt and was "practically indestructible" during transit. Today, Necco Sweethearts are perhaps the most iconic Valentine's Day heart-shaped sweet, bearing a variety of printed messages suitable for the holiday: "Be Mine", "Kiss Me", "Call Me", " Let's Get Busy", or "Miss You". The paper wrapping is nearly unchanged in 153 years as is the candy itself. Its cylindrical package is still a dusty deck of colorful discs, each stamped with the Necco name. Holding a package, one can imagine how the candy was a great come-on to deliver medicine to recalcitrant children.

An era ended in 2003 when the Necco factory moved from Cambridge to the nearby suburb of Revere, Massachusetts. That climaxed a period that the *Cambridge Chronicle* highlighted in 1905, proudly claiming, "Cambridge has come to be one of the greatest confectionery manufacturing cities of the United States." That was in an article describing the Lydian Confectionery Company that had a 10 H.P. engine to propel its equipment. Lydian produced hard candies, their so-called winter goods, to be had at railroad stations, leading drug stores, hotels, and confectionery establishments where "strictly high-grade confections were in demand". Their Other or Summer specialties included the famous *Silverettes*. Lydian merged with Imperial Chocolates and the two were eventually merged with Daggett. Any Silverettes today are only "made in Italy by actual silversmiths" to use as nursing cups. To be fair, there's also The Silverettes, the real rock'n roll chicks, or the dance line with the same name that performs routines with the Northern Illinois Huskie Marching Band.

An enrober machine to coat chocolate bars

7. Candy Making Machines

At the turn of the 19th century, candy was still made in domestic kitchens, and, Dover Stamping and Manufacturing on Putnam Avenue in Cambridgeport helped homemakers with their Famous Dover Egg Beater that was fabricated from galvanized sheet metal. This simple hand tool made it easier to combine eggs, milk, cream and other ingredients in a confectionery mix. It was produced by a one-of-a-kind company. Dover's production facilities were an interesting contrast to the foundries and machine shops that together constituted the largest single industry in 1905 Cambridge. Their most successful products were the machine tools that supplemented and even replaced the handwork needed to manufacture consumable goods. Generic machine tools were born when the machine itself guided the toolpath, minimizing the need for hand guidance in the cutting or forming process. With the advent of the steam engine, power-driven machines were able to produce material goods. One of the first to develop an idea for a machine that would make it possible to produce those goods in a continuing process was the same Oliver Evans that first built a high-pressure, non-condensing reciprocating engine. Without formal training, Evans automated his brother's flour mill, becoming one of the first to design a repetitive manufacturing system that didn't involve human labor. Machines like his, in turn, had been fabricated by machine tools able to produce dimensionally accurate parts in large quantities. Mass production with interchangeable parts had become a reality.

Having such advances to work with, an English druggist and the founder of Necco, Oliver R. Chase, patented his ground-breaking lozenge-making machine in 1883.8. Candy Making Machines in 1883.

Oliver Chase lozenge making machines

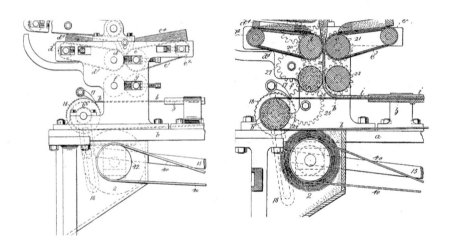

Chase's machine could replace the often sticky process of hand-making medicinal lozenges and it was the precursor of dozens of candy types that are still popular today. Belts driven by a steam engine were connected to drive wheels at each end of his machine that in turn drove geared parts to produce individual small, round sweets from raw materials.

The process started when a supply of sugar paste was loaded from the top into rollers that shaped the material into a continuous band of uniform thickness. Bins from the side added a coating of flour or powdered starch to prevent the band from sticking. The no nearly dry band was fed through planishing or bright rolls and it landed on a continuously rotating carrier belt that carried it to an assembly that divided the band into uniform sections and punched out the finished lozenges, which then nicely dropped into a receiving bin. As Chase's pharmacy grew into the New England Confectionery Company, it used a similar machine to produce the thinner *Necco Wafers*. The *enrober* machine for coating a sweet substance with chocolate was invented in 1903 by Messrs. Savy Jeanjean & Co. of Paris and imported by Cambridge candy makers to produce bars like *Snickers* and *Milky Way*. *British and American* inventors eventually improved on the French machine, but there were few applications actually patented. Improvements in the machinery came along rapidly, so it was seldom worth justifying the time and expense in securing new patents. Patenting a name, a wrapper, and a logo made more sense; but the recipes and ingredients were fair game, making it possible for a competitor to sell a copycat of your product. Additionally, the staple ingredients of most candies were quite similar and thus hard to patent, so differences in the mix or quantities in the manufacturing were sealed in the minds of the processors and passed down when personnel changed.

It appears that candy makers didn't record any patents after the original Chase's lozenge filing until 1924, when William S. Cloud of the Euclid Candy Company in Cleveland filed a patent for a system used to make the *Love Nest* bar.

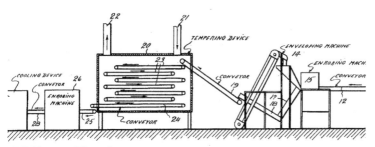

William Cloud Diagram in Patent Application 1924

The Love Nest patent application stated that the invention's object was to provide a continuous process for manufacturing confections, "so that it was unnecessary to handle the same from the time the centers or uncoated pieces were fed to the machine until they were rejected as finished confections ready for wrapping and boxing, thereby materially expediting the production of the confections and effecting a large saving in the cost of making the same." Another object of the Love Nest machine was to provide a "continuous process whereby more uniform and better grade confections were produced than was possible by the hand

process that involved considerable handling of the pieces."
The continuous process included steps of feeding
previously prepared articles through a tempering device to
condition the same and then through an enrobing device to
coat the conditioned pieces with a finished material.
Finally, the coated pieces were cooled and then wrapped
and boxed. In detail, the device coated all surfaces with
the same viscous 4g material such as caramel, then
enveloped the coated centers with a multiplicity of edible
units such as peanuts, tempering the pieces thus formed,
then enrobed the tempered pieces with a coating of
finishing material such as chocolate

A Manual brake.

8. Biscuits & Bread

Thomas S. Ollive was Vice President of *Nabisco*, the baking conglomerate whose merger of 114 firms included the Kennedy Biscuit Company on Franklin Street in Cambridge. In 1916, Ollive wrote his reminiscences of growing up with the also Revolution, he was an immigrant that left England in 1845 for the United States and New York City, where his father started a small cracker factory. Oliive tells how there were only eight cracker makers in that city. All made similar products, except for Joseph Bruen, who would personally deliver his fresh-baked oyster crackers to customers from his two-wheeled cart while wearing a long tailcoat and silk hat. Then, crude machines cut pilot or soda crackers from rolled dough, but other flat items like sugar crackers, or cookies, were produced with hand labor in a wooden trough. The dough from the trough that had been covered with a canvas cloth was treaded into a solid mass and then taken to a circular platform called the *brake* where a man jumped up and down on a long stick attached to an iron swivel to knead the dough into the right consistency.

Ollive went west to California where he made pilot crackers for sea voyagers, but returned to New York in 1860, where he opened his own shop making the hardtack for soldiers in the Civil War. During the decade, baking machinery improved and the first dough-making machines were imported from England. In the U.S., D. M. Holmes invented a machine that cut soft dough into segments. Automation in every sector of the food industry was improving as the inventors and tool-makers became more adept at reducing the grunt-work. Nowhere in the U.S. was there a greater concentration of both machine makers and bakery producers than in East Cambridge and Kendall Square. The net result, of course, of any labor-saving device was a loss in demand for those skilled in the process whose labors were lost. Innovation and machine fabrication meant a kind of by unemployment at the turn of the 19th century, just as it does with those who lose jobs to robots and sophisticated machines today. Around 1900, however, the genius of men like Alexander Graham Bell, Thomas Edison, Rudolph Diesel, Willis Carrier, and King Gillette kept creating new fields to employ those no longer needed in defunct industrial roles.

*The Holmes Dough
Cutting Machine*

Towards the end of the 19th century, bakers near Kendall Square in Cambridge were independent operators like the Swedish Bakery on Main Street. Established in 1888, the bakery claimed to be "the largest place in the eastern states engaged in the manufacture of Swedish baked goods." A 30 horsepower electric motor operated machinery to produce "everything that can be termed Swedish bake stuffs." Their specialty was Petterson's famous Swedish Health Bread, named after owner Oscar G. Petterson. He sold the "stuffs" in Pennsylvania, Minnesota, and other sections of the country with considerable Swedish populations. Over on Franklin Street, the Kennedy Biscuit Company had been founded by Artemas Kennedy in the 1850's. Using a family recipe, Artemas, found he could control the fermentation that occurred when yeast, dough, and water were mixed together and came up with crackers called the *Kennedy Commons,* which were so popular they eventually found their way to the larders of California gold diggers. After that came pretzels, gingersnaps, and zwiebacks and then the *Fig Newton,* a soft cookie filled with jam. They'd purchased the idea from its originator Charles M. Roser, an Ohio baker. Some claimed that Roser had named his specialty after the famous Sir Isaac, but Frank A. Kennedy insisted it was named after the nearby Boston suburb of Newton. He named all of his products after surrounding communities, selling cookies and crackers called *Shrewsbury, Harvard,* and *Beacon Hill.* Producing a cookie filled with jam could have been a sticky business, but Kennedy used a machine invented by James Henry Mitchell where an inside funnel pumped out the jam and an outside funnel pumped out the dough to produce an endless roll that was then cut into smaller pieces. Frank A. Kennedy's Fig Newtons were some of the first cookies to be mass-produced; and, adding to his accomplishments, he was the first to produce *Boston Baked Beans* in a hermetically sealed can. The company used innovative processors like reel ovens, which used a Ferris wheel type of mechanism to control cooking of the products. By 1889, with a staff of 650, it was the largest baking operation in the country.

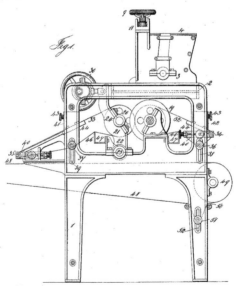

The Mitchell machine

Corporations began to replace the mom-and-pop bakeries. The mechanization of what was once a muscle-intensive operation allowed bakers in Cambridge to operate at lower costs and make it possible to sell their wares outside of the immediate area. C. F. Hathaway & Son, Wholesale Bakers, turned out a product like *Hathaway's Celebrated Cream Bread* at a price that precluded the necessity for home baking. Their Massachusetts Avenue plant had seven ovens that they claimed could do the work of ten ordinary ovens, using over a carload of flour per week. On State Street, R. Megson & Co. announced that their *Little Wonder* cake machines were so advanced that "fully one thousand high-priced cake bakers and confectioners all over the world had lost their positions," because they were replaced by Megson's patented invention that could deposit, distribute, and cut cake dough to make 25,000 cakes an hour. It's probable that Reed's Pearl Street Bakery didn't use the machine, because in only six years the staff increased from two to sixteen without using a Megson machine. Reed's specialty was home-delivery; but his bake-stuffs were so popular that Yerxa & Yerxa installed a special Reed's booth in their Central Square grocery store that boasted, "Having the best facilities for the quick delivery of orders, this firm enjoys a large telephone trade with the best families within a big radius, and the only aim of Woodford Yerxa is to endeavor to please his patrons."

Conglomerates began to compete with and

eventually absorb the smaller bakers. Founded in 1849, Ward Baking Company became Continental Baking Company in 1925, and the founder's grandson, William Ward, took over. Ward soon added Taggart Baking, makers of the ubiquitous and still extant *Wonder Bread* that Taggart had launched in 1921 with a come-on advertising promotion that touted a *Wonder* bread long before it appeared on grocery shelves. It would be "Soon Available!" Princeton graduate Elmer Cline, a vice-president of the company, claimed that the bread's name came to him while he watched the International Balloon Race in Indianapolis. "I was filled with *Wonder*." The array of colors Cline saw in the racing balloons ended up on the bread's logo. This was the age of slogans, when Continental's mainstay product became " Slo-baked" and "The greatest thing since sliced bread." Actually, they temporarily dropped the claim when a shortage of slicer steel prompted an industry-wide practice that left Wonder bread unsliced for a few months during World War II. Continuing mergers, the Continental company added Hall Baking Company and the Paniplus Company to its holdings and the name *Hostess* to its cake products. Besides Cambridge, it had factories in Providence, The Bronx, Baltimore, Pittsburgh, and Cleveland producing its *Twinkies*.

The conglomerate National Biscuit Company, *Nabisco*, began modestly in 1792 as Pearson & Sons in

Massachusetts. They made their *Pilot Bread* or hardtack, the only baked product rugged enough to survive and be consumed on long sea voyages. In 1889, William Moore acquired Pearson and combined it with seven other bakeries to start the New York Biscuit Company. Concurrently, Adolphus Green, born in Boston, Harvard graduate, one of eleven children and for a brief time headmaster of the Groton School, created the American Biscuit & Manufacturing Company. Eight years later, Moore joined attorney Green and they merged New York Biscuit and the large Kennedy Biscuit Company of Cambridge with more than 100 other bakeries to create the National Biscuit Company. This added Kennedy Biscuit's *Fig Newtons* and *Lorna Doones* to the product line. One of those in the merger, The S.S. Marvin Co. was created in Pittsburgh by Sylvester S. Marvin, who was known as the Edison of the industry because of his innovative manufacturing ideas. Of interest in a broader sense, all this happened in spite of the Sherman Anti-Trust Act that became law in 1890.

Adolphus Green was elected president of the new multi-state company; and, as president, he encouraged employees to buy company stock and he refused to hire children. While other bakers traditionally sold their product in bulk, Green introduced biscuits that were packaged in a folded wax paper and cardboard container called *In-Er-Seal,* that was assured to "seal in the flavor." The many-faceted National Biscuit Company finally reduced its name to *Nabisco,* and the acronym still appears all over the world on *Oreo* cookies, a name that has prompted many theories about its source. The simplest: *Or* in French means "gold" and the original products were packaged in gold. Next: *Oreo* in Greek means "beautiful" or "nice." Then: *Oros* in Greek means " mountain" or "hill" and the first cookies were mounded with a hill in the center. Truly: no one seems to know. The interesting end of the Nabisco story is that both the cookie and the company name survived, despite the possibility of it being lost in one of the largest leveraged buyouts in history when R.J. Reynolds purchased the company. Then Reynolds sold it to **Philip Morris Companies Inc.** who merged it with **Kraft Foods**, one of the largest mergers in the food industry. In 2011, Kraft Foods announced it was splitting, making the snack-food business a separate company to be called **Mondelēz International LLC.** If you are looking to munch on one of Mondelēz's Oreos today, you'll find it's been baked in Canada, Mexico, Indonesia, India, China, Pakistan, Spain, or Russia; but apparently not in the USA. The Chicago plant was closed down in 2016.

The Cambridge of eighteen hundred and ninety-six, edited by Arthur Gilman in 1896, described the changes under way in the baking industry.

> Those not familiar with the methods practiced in a well-equipped modern bakery have but little idea of the extent to which machinery is used, or of the great

changes that have been wrought by it in the baker's art since the days of our grandfathers. Then the skill of an operative lay in his ability to turn out a small quantity and a very limited variety of goods with his own hands, and such simple hand implements as are familiar to all good housewives. Today there is little, and in most bakeries no hand work done, and the skill of a mechanic lies in his knowledge of the machines, and how to get from them the largest amount and the highest quality of goods they are capable of producing.

9. Baking Machines

A tombstone from ancient Rome describes Seanatore Eurysace as a prominent baker of the day. The hard work of kneading his dough was assigned to slaves who wore gloves as a safeguard against spreading germs. In 1902, Emil Brown's *The Baker's Handbook* described how a dough-making machine became preferred because of its cleanliness. Further:

> It costs very little to feed, it does not smoke or chew, and, as for the can, it only needs a small one filled with oil. It is always willing and never shirks the work, don't get tired, and never goes on a strike: in fact it is an ideal worker.

This was certainly true for the large bakers in the Kendall Square corridor; but even housewives were being encouraged to use machines at home to make biscuits and bread. Dough mixing and kneading was hard and time-consuming work for busy mothers and Landers, Frary & Clark in New Britain Connecticut patented a machine in 1903 to ease the process.

Landers, Frary & Clark
Homemaker
Bread Machine

Landers, Frary & Clark Homemaker Bread Machine ad:

> Very simple in construction. A child can operate it. As easily cleaned as a tin pail. We guarantee this simple machine to Mix and Knead Bread perfectly in 3 minutes. You need not get your fingers "all stuck up" with Dough. Or worry about Bread Making any more. The "Universal" Three Minute Bread Maker is Mixer, Kneader and Raiser, all combined.

Landers Frary and Clark were only following the trend set for commercial bakeries, who had been using machines for some time. As early as 1831 at Carlisle, England, Jonathon Carr invented a biscuit-cutting machine that acted like a printing press. Around 1850, there were great developments in dough mixing machines and new types of biscuit cutters. Actually, some of the machinery workings followed smaller models used in domestic kitchens: the eggbeater just got much bigger and the bowl doubled in size. In contrast to how things worked in a home kitchen, however, mass production meant the process had to be continuous; and, with baked goods, it meant abandoning the "rest" that dough got between manual handlings. It's believed the rest gave the gluten a chance to "relax" and limited it's tendency to resist the spring as the bread entered the final process of baking. When it came to that baking, mechanization wasn't far behind the dough mixer. In 1853, New Yorker Hosea Ball invented a baking oven with a horizontal shaft. As the shaft was turned, it rotated a circular rack holding four loaves of dough, making it possible to move each of them through the oven and to deliver the finished product where it could be easily removed through the oven's front door.

The Hosea Ball Baking Oven

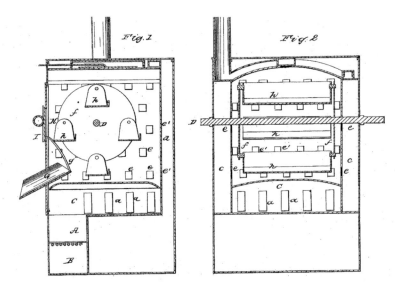

Like the candy makers, many biscuit makers found that their machines were being constantly improved and patents were seldom worth the time and money it took to obtain them. Product identity became more important. Kennedy Bakery secured Trade Marks on four different items in a single year, while Daniel. M. Holmes needed that entire year to finally receive a patent in 1881 for a machine to crimp the sheets of dough before they were cut into cakes.

D. M. Holmes Machine for Crimping Dough

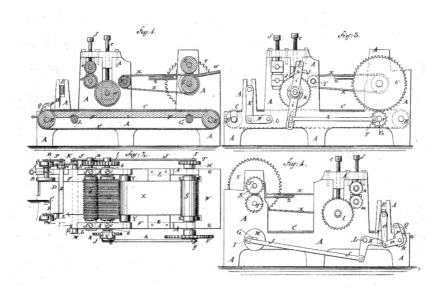

There were patents for machines that changed the basic baking process, however, that were worth taking the time to obtain. Holmes machine was one. It somewhat resembled Chase's lozenge maker in that the raw dough material was fed in from above and then through rollers that smoothed it into a sheet. The sheet was fed onto a continuously rolling belt and passed between two crimping-rollers placed at different levels and in such positions that their faces could be brought into contact with each other, or nearly so, allowing the sheet to be crimped on one or both sides. After the crimping, the sheet dropped to another continuously rolling belt that delivered the material to the cutters and thence to a receiving box. Like Holmes, J.R. Farmer found it worthwhile in 1900 to patent his invention of a machine that improved the dough mixing process.

J. R. Farmer
Dough Mixer

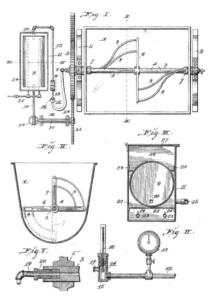

In an attempt to offset the lack of the "rest" introduced by mechanization, Farmer's mixer injected air into the mixing trough. A thermometer measured temperature of the mix, and the air could be heated by gas or cooled by passing it through an ice-box. Farmer's complicated way of mixing dough was soon changed by an engineer for the Hobart Manufacturing Company named Herbert Johnson, who invented an electric standing mixer in 1908. His inspiration came from observing a baker mixing bread dough with a metal spoon. Soon he was toying with a mechanical counterpart. By 1915, his 80-quart mixer was standard equipment for most large bakeries. In a reverse of how most baking machines were developments of hand-held domestic instruments, the Hobart Mix Master was downsized for home use and is still popular with earnest home bakers. Kendall Square also had a source for dough mixers. Barbour Stockwell advertised their Boston Mixer in 1903 that was made in five sizes for the "mixing of pastes, doughs and other ingredients." The machine was almost too successful. Contractors in Massachusetts were using the same machine to mix sand and gravel on roadway projects.

The ultimate patent in the 1900's baking world was awarded to a Hungarian in Indiana named Christian Kessler. Kessler invented an "automatic" bread making machine that took the pre-mixed dough at one end and produced oven-ready loaves at the other. The pre-mix was dumped into a large hopper and then made into a uniformly sized sheet. The sheet was coated with dry flour and passed onto a continuous belt, sent through a forming die, then divided into parts or loaves of equal size and weight ready to be placed in the baking oven. In this case, the support framework was cast in a foundry; but the many moving parts had to be precisely cut by skilled machinists. This was a case where the machinists were critical in the production of a machine tool, producing a more compact, integrated product.

Kessler "Automatic" Bread Making Machine

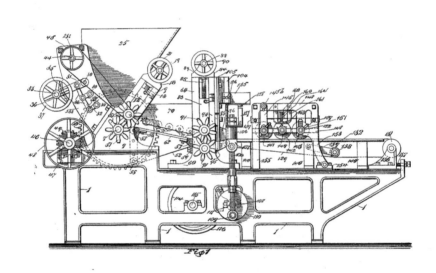

10. Soap

The ancients cleaned up using certain plant juices and fuller's earth, which they spread over a garment and then forced in by stamping their feet. According to the historian Pliny, however, making something to ease the washing process began with the Gauls. They were the original soap makers. The Romans adopted the concept, combining wood ashes of the beech tree and fat from rendered goats and an example of one of the Roman shops where they concocted the soap still can be seen in the ruins of Pompeii. The process evolved so that by the 8th century both Italy and Spain were making soap. In France, the first soap manufacturer set up shop in Marseilles, where olive oil was abundant and could be mixed with crude soda extracted from maritime kelp and seaweed. When these two elements were boiled, the foam formed at the top was scraped off as soap. Across the channel, the English followed the French system with Jones and Palmer receiving the first English patent for manufacturing what they called *sape*. And in America, the first official indication of the use of soap came with President George Washington's signature on two soap-related documents issued to John Nazro. One was a patent that protected his method of making soap. A second covered the extraction of alkali from seaweed, similar to the French process, providing an alternative to wood ash as one of the basic ingredients in soap production. Then, in 1807, Sir Benjamin Thompson, an American born in Woburn, Massachusetts whose numerous scientific discoveries including the modern fireplace garnered him the English title of Count Rumford, found that injecting steam into the soap making process reduced the operation time from to sixty to six hours. By 1884 in England, Alexander Watt, had amassed knowledge of still more production methods and he described many significant changes in *The Art of Soap-Making:*

The next great discovery was due to another French chemist, Chevreul, who raised soap-making from empiricism and rule-of- thumb guesswork to its present exalted position as a truly scientific art. With the rapid advance of chemical knowledge… the art of soap-making gradually improved, and many saponifiable substances were introduced from time to time, until, at the present day, the lengthy list includes oils and other fatty matters which were never dreamed of by our forefathers. It would not be incorrect, however, to say that up to forty years ago soap manufacture was generally conducted without any reference to scientific principles or chemical theories.

Although new machines were reducing the required amount of hand labor, men and women were still sweating in Kendall Square factories where hundreds of humans were concentrated without air-conditioning, and in homes where bathing still was a weekly event. Of course the effects of such conditions were mitigated by those machines that made it possible to produce soaps in quantity, varying shapes, and multiple varieties. Soaps were a demand product. In the simplest terms, soap at the turn of the century was a combination of natural oils, lye (an alkali solution rich in potassium or sodium hydroxide) and animal fats. As a place rich in these fats, East Cambridge was an excellent location for many soap makers, because of the nearby pork rendering facilities at the John P. Squire & Co. that manufactured *Extra Lard Oil* on a twenty acre site along Gore Street.

The soap business started in Cambridge around 1804 with Nathaniel Livermore on Main Street and E.A.&W. Winchester, a butcher who used leftover fats to make his soap. Their products were shipped from Cambridgeport to as far away as the Caribbean and even South America. Norton's Soap Works opened in 1820 and produced *Norton's Tidy Soap* until a fire wiped out the premises in 1902. Valentine Soap Co. opened its doors in 1828 on the corner of Valentine and Pearl streets, which neighbors nicknamed "Greasy Village," because of the odoriferous setting. As an incentive to attract and keep employees, Valentine erected two houses on Cottage Street to house his workers. The houses remain today and are listed on the National Register of Historic Places. Another soap maker, Lysander Kemp & Sons, founded in 1850, had a three-story building at the corner of Broadway and Davis streets.

Kemp was followed in 1856 by John Reardon, who formed a company to manufacture candles and soaps in nearby Cambridgeport. In 1863, the firm name was permanently changed to John Reardon & Sons Company. As the use of candles declined, Reardon began to specialize in laundry and toiletry soaps. In 1878, the company moved to a larger factory in the area around Fort Washington and began manufacturing glycerin, an ingredient that gave soap more clarity. At its height, Reardon employed 150 workers. To produce the soaps used by many of the leading hotels, laundries and institutions around Boston and vicinity, all of these companies used clear water obtained from two artesian wells going down 452 feet and 552 feet respectively.

In the Castile region of Spain, they produced a soap made out of vegetable oils, probably the first white soap ever made. Although the Spanish produced and promoted the use of their soap, in 17th century England the Catholic Church had a monopoly on Castile, bringing protests from the Protestant population and the eventual loss of exclusivity for the Catholics. In 1881, Frank H. Teele started Teele Soap Company in 1881 to produce a soap in a style similar to that made in Castile. Another Cambridge soap maker was *C. L. Jones & Co.'s* with a manufacturing plant at the corner of Pearl and Valentine Streets that started producing soap in 1845. They advertised their wares with Victorian Trade Cards showing well-scrubbed children. Cherubic babies were shown holding what could have been soap molded to look like small dolls. Their soap, popular throughout New England and New York State, was made in ten huge kettles with a united capacity of 400,000 pounds. Two twenty-five horsepower engines energized the process. Although C. L. Jones shut down in 1902, their trade cards remain collector's items today.

The biggest soap maker in Cambridge, in fact in all of Massachusetts, was located on Broadway in the Kendall Square corridor. It was Lever Brothers, a branch of a parent company that had been manufacturing soap in England since William Hesketh Lever and James Darcy Lever founded it in the 1870's, utilizing a new soap-making process invented by chemist William Hough Watson that contained glycerin and vegetable oils such as palm oil, rather than tallow. By the 1880's, the company had experienced significant success from its product line and began expanding production to meet international demands. To create an American base, William Lever established the Cambridge subsidiary in 1898 by purchasing the Curtis Davis Company, which had been established in 1835 and was known for its *Welcome* brand of soap. During its initial years in Cambridge, the Lever Brothers Company saw slow and steady growth. Despite the success of the company's *Sunlight* and *Lifebuoy* brands overseas, the firm was unable to replicate those sales in the United States, so they turned to the *Welcome* soap brand they'd inherited from the Curtis

Davis Company for their initial sales effort. In 1913, however, the firm began to see significant growth in U.S. sales, and the company initiated a series of American-focused marketing campaigns. They eliminated production of *Sunlight* soap and focused on promoting *the Lux, Rinso, Welcome*, and *Lifebuoy* brands to the American public. As sales in the United States kept rising, by 1929, Lever Brothers was the third-largest soap manufacturer in the country, employing approximately 1,000 workers in its Cambridge plant that filled two blocks on Broadway, just above the Kendall Square depot.

11: Soap Making Machines

The first Soap manufacturer in the United States was Colgate & Company that started making soap in New York in the early 1800's in a huge kettle holding 45,000 pounds of their product. In 1873, Colgate introduced a second product, toothpaste, sold in jars until they found a method to pack it in tubes where it could be applied directly to a toothbrush. In 1928, the firm was purchased by Palmolive-Peet to create the Colgate-Palmolive Company. Rival Proctor and Gamble was founded by candle maker William Proctor and soap maker James Gamble after their mutual father-in-law, Alexander Morris, suggested that both products needed lye and the two should combine forces. This happened in 1837 Cincinnati, nicknamed *Porkopolis* because of its large hog-butchering industry. Given this ideal source of fats, the new Proctor & Gamble firm soon focused on soap making. Their product line changed after a worker accidentally left a soap mixer running during a lunch break and added more air than usual to the mix, after which P&G could feature the miracle of a floating *Ivory* soap. As an alternative to the others, the Palmolive company manufactured soap made entirely from palm and olive oils. They began advertising their product in the 1920's on radio programs, such as *Kay Kyser's Kollege of Musical Knowledge*, whose airwave shows resulted in the term *soap opera* being added to the common vernacular.

Before the Second Industrial Revolution, mixing oil and an alkali together and pouring the liquid into a mold to make soap didn't take the most sophisticated equipment. All they needed were the basic ingredients and a batch kettle for boiling. Around the turn of the century, although others were inventing ways to mass-produce consumer goods, they were still making soap with simple, separate pieces of equipment, often still hand-operated. It took until 1930 for Proctor & Gamble to devise a continuous process that decreased production time for making soap to less than a day. Their system utilized some of the ideas advanced by Count Rumford and also an Englishman named Robert Freeland, who was living in Boston and received three patents in 1882, 1884 and 1889. One was a patent for a soap-making machine that improved the mixing process by using curved mixer blades on a central revolving shaft. Technically called a *crutcher,* the shaft sat in a tank surrounded by coiled tubing that could be used to heat or cool the contents.

Freeland Soap
Making Machine

As the art of soap-making improved, machines were invented to handle each successive step in the process. The first stage required a soap saponification machine, which was basically the large batch kettle where raw materials were boiled to remove impurities. The next in line was a mixer that combined a variety of additives with raw soap to produce a hard paste. In 1900, two Germans from Hamburg, Charles Culmann and Carl Witter, were granted a United States patent for " A soap-making machine, comprising a vessel, a pair of concentric bells therein, communication between the interior of said bells near the top, and means to move the contents of the vessel to the top of the inner bell, substantially as and for the purpose set forth."

Witter Soap Making Machine

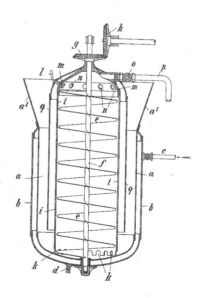

After the soap set up into a hard paste, it could be pressed
into bars with machines like the one manufactured by
Baker Perkins in England.

Baker Perkins
Toilet Soap
Machine

With the stamping machine, soap producers had the chance
to create a distinctive shape and press an identifying name
into the product: *Ivory, Lifebuoy, Palmolive*.

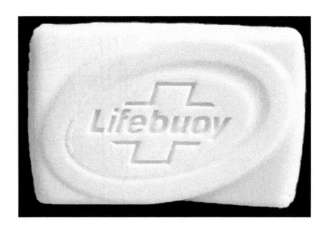

As techniques improved, a Vacuum Plodder was developed to extrude a long continuous billet of the hardening paste. The billets were then fed into a Cutting Machine. One of the earliest versions was invented by Williams, Warner, Springer, and Aydelott in 1901. "This invention relates to improvements in two parallel slots 1 and 2, which form guides machines for cutting slabs of soap into cakes for the bars 3 and 4, which have a sliding fit and for automatically separating the cakes therein."

Williams, Warner, Springer & Aydelott Cutting Machine

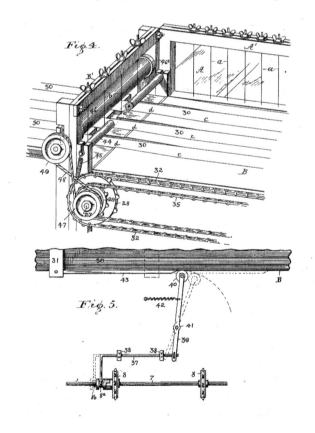

At Lever Brothers in Cambridge they were using similar equipment, often repeats of the machines used at the parent company in England. More than patents on machinery, they were interested in protecting their innovations in the materials used to make soap. Importantly, there were distinct differences in the *Toilet* products used at home and those labeled *Laundry*. Thus, just in one year,1899, Lever Brothers applied for three different Toilet patents in November and December and three different Laundry patents in June and November. Their Patent Number 33,945 was issued to secure the rights to use a picture of a swan as an advertising symbol for a toilet soap. One of their more interesting patents was for equipment to produce a floating toilet soap in 1935, a latter day attempt to compete with Proctor and Gamble's *Ivory* soap.

Alexander Watt in his *The Art of Soap-Making,* described how the French had introduced chemistry into the soap-making equation, he couldn't have conceived of the changes that would come about in 1916, when the first synthetic detergent was developed in Germany in response to a shortage of any kind of fats during World War 1. Although the idea wasn't immediately incorporated in soaps, similar shortages in World War II prompted a change to such detergents that carried over into America. In 1946, soap manufacturers began to substitute a mixture of synthetic chemicals to produce a soap that would finally replace ones made from glycerin and vegetable oils that in themselves had replaced animal fat and soda ash. Although the first detergents were used primarily for washing hands and fine fabrics, the breakthrough in using detergents for all-purpose laundry work came in 1946 when the first "built" detergent (containing a *surfactant/builder* combination) was introduced in the U.S. The *surfactant*'s molecules helped water to get hold of grease, break it up, and wash it away, while the *builder* helped the surfactant to work more efficiently. By 1953, sales of the new detergents in this country had surpassed those of conventionally produced soap.

12. Transit

The Second Industrial Revolution that saw production of hundreds of labor-saving machines in the Kendall Square corridor also had unintended consequences. Those that purchased the new machines were delighted with the increased productivity and they soon realized that concentrating men and machines under one factory roof near a central source of power increased profitability. All these new workers needed places to live and developers answered with new construction. While the clustering of mill buildings and housing produced an overall efficiency, the influx of all these new people crowded the much-too-narrow existing streets. Roger N. Parks described conditions along these now heavily trafficked routes in *Roads in New England, 1790-1840*, published by Old Sturbridge Village in 1965.

> The main street at the beginning of the nineteenth century was likely to be littered with "fragments of old fences, boards, clapboards, wood piles, heaps of chips, old sleds bottom upwards, carts, casks, weeds and loose stones, lying along in wild confusion," while the roadway itself was "scandalously bad; foot ways, or cross paths, ruts and gutters, with stones at every step, disturb the traveler in his carriage, and the teamsters with their loads."

Those that couldn't pay for carriages looked eagerly for affordable ways to rise above the roadway clutter. In 1880, John Kemp Stanley invented the first "safety bicycle" that had a steerable front wheel and a chain drive to operate the rear wheel

Then John Dunlop bonded canvas with liquid rubber and produced the first pneumatic tire, so cyclists could be literally riding on air. In 1887 dedicated bike riders founded the Cambridgeport Cycle Club. This was just one recognition of the fact that the bicycle was indeed a reasonable departure from man's use of his legs or use of an animal-driven vehicle. It was true that the bicycle got people from one point to another; but, whether one used it or still rode in a carriage, the trips were bumpy and often interrupted by stalled carriages or loose debris.

There was a solution to the problem of inadequate roadbeds. It grew out of an industrial source in 1826 when the Granite Railway Company, the first to be so chartered, was opened to transport granite from Quincy to

Charlestown, Massachusetts. The new railway was installed to furnish the stone that was needed to complete the Bunker Hill Monument. In nearby Cambridge, entrepreneurs wanted to adapt the granite railway idea to transport people. In 1853, they chartered the new Cambridge Railroad to connect the West End of Boston with Central and Harvard squares in Cambridge. At the time, as with the Granite Railway, the Cambridge Railroad used horse-drawn cars to carry passengers along the tracks laid down along main streets. The method of propulsion changed in 1887 after the West End Street Railway consolidated ownership of a number of the horse-drawn streetcar lines in Boston and the inner suburbs and created a fleet with 7816 horses and 1480 rail vehicles. They began converting their animal-drawn vehicles to electric propulsion in 1889, but were briefly stopped over a controversy. At issue was the best way to move the railway cars. Should they simply install overhead wires to provide electric power or should the system be switched to use underground, pulled-cable propulsion, similar to that used with cable cars in San Francisco? The latter system was visually cleaner, but after a team of horses was electrocuted during a run on a test track that used the underground cable, the West End Street Railway settled on overhead wires. The electric power for the overhead wires came from an industry that was in its infancy in the late 19th century. There was no AC or alternating current power grid as we know it today. The first electric streetcar lines were powered by DC electricity, whose limited transmission range required multiple power plants in downtown Boston, Allston, Cambridge (near Harvard), Dorchester, Charlestown, East Cambridge, and East Boston. The difficulty of transporting large quantities of coal from the Port of Boston to service those multiple power plant locations added to the short range of the DC system and discouraged significant expansion elsewhere.

On September 30,1892, Massachusetts had 814 miles of street railway, 492 miles of which were powered by electricity. The aggregate patronage exceeded 193,000,000. By 1904, a good share of the state's totals could be found in the Greater Boston West End Street Railway system, which had 36 megawatts of generating capacity, owned 1550 streetcars (mostly closed but some open) and included 421 miles of track. Although the DC current was still a limiting factor in overall operations, the introduction of the metal rails greatly enhanced ridership because there was less rolling resistance than that found on even the best laid granite block or macadam paving. The electric streetcars were a definite step up from the old horsebus. They were faster, more sanitary and with a lower epizootic risk, cheaper to run, and without the cost of excreta cleanup and the ultimate disposal of horse carcasses. Now happy passengers could make the trip oblivious to "fragments of old fences, boards, clapboards, etc."

As a new mode of transportation, street railways inevitably had their share of financial and political issues. Streetcars paid business and property taxes and often were hit with franchise fees. Many franchise fees were fixed, or were based on the gross, not the net income. Taxing the rail lines didn't recognize the fact that they maintained the rights of way that they shared with other vehicles and provided street sweeping and snow clearance. The railways were also required to maintain minimal, often uneconomic, service levels.. In order to reach agreements with respective communities, the railways had to schedule unreasonable trips and stops. Added to this, a holdover from earlier days, when horse-drawn vehicles required a two-man crew, created financial problems in later years as salaries outpaced revenues. As with every new enterprise that matures, employees began asking for an increase in wages, as discussed in The *Street Railway Review* of 1891.

They are convinced that the company is earning unduly large dividends…and should therefore divide these profits with them. Yet even were the companies making more than enough to meet fixed charges, the employees have no right to assume they are entitled to the excess. There is no special reason for granting them increased wages or reduced hours of work, so long as the company can hire all the men it wants at less wages than those now given.

The Review argued further that, while in the days of horse-car transportation the cost of accidents to horses could be very closely anticipated, with the advent of modern electric vehicles "The liability is that almost any morning the manager may wake up to learn that during the night someone has discovered an improvement in electric railway appliances which renders some part of his equipment obsolete. So rapid have been the improvements marking the last three years…that many roads have thrown out more than they have worn out."

Horse drawn trolley on the Cambridge Railroad

13: Frogs and Sprockets

On September 9, 1905, the *Cambridge Chronicle* declared that:

> Ever since the street railway business was established in Boston, Cambridge has enjoyed superior service. The first horse car line operated in New England was between Cambridge and Boston. The first complete trolley line in New England was between Harvard Square and Boston: the first subway that will connect Boston with any suburb will undoubtedly soon be built in Cambridge.

Cambridge and Kendall Square companies were prepared to make all those products that the new street railways required, particularly the constant improvements in tracks and the replacement parts needed after travel over the switches wore them out. The railway track business could be lucrative. One mile of track required 352 pieces of rail thirty feet long.

Historically, the first rails used to guide horse-driven wagons were carved out of wood. These were superseded by metal-capped wood, then cast iron rails that could be shaped but that had to be made in short lengths and were brittle and easily broken. Bethlehem Steel rolled the first steel rails in 1863 and supplied the bulk of the rails used to build US railroads until Carnegie Steel and other Pittsburgh mills began to offer competitive prices in the 1880's. In 1908, out of 14 rolling mills in Massachusetts, there were none in Cambridge that specialized in manufacturing steel rails. Cambridge firms were, however, making the critical parts involved in switching a train from one set of rails to another. The industry had its own technical terms. *Frogs* made it possible to switch from one track to the other and *Sprockets* were the cogged wheels used in the switches.

When the Cambridge Railroad was built in 1853, Allen & Endicott, were called upon to furnish a large part of the track material used. The building of other roads rapidly followed, and the activity in this field added a permanent and important branch to their already large and successful business. Allen & Endicott eventually became Alfred Morrill & Co., and when Barbour Stockwell & Co. absorbed that firm, it continued manufacturing special railroad rails, frogs, and switches. Various causes combined to bring about a rapid increase in the volume of business after the consolidation. A large part of the increase was due to the impetus given to street railway construction by the introduction of electricity as a motive power. With the new system, heavier cars were brought into use, and the old track, which had been good enough for horse-car service, was found to be too light for the heavier cars and their increased speed. It soon became necessary to replace all the tracks with heavier rail, and new and improved special parts replaced the old as rapidly as they could be procured and laid.

One of the larger jobs undertaken by Barbour Stockwell was furnishing the curves, frogs and switches for an electric railroad in Austin, Texas. They were ordered by a Kansas developer named Monroe Shipe, who had acquired a large plot of land north of Austin that he grandly dubbed *Hyde Park.* Knowing that the land was too far outside of town to attract the wealthy buyers he sought, Shipe secured a franchise for an Austin Rapid Transit Railway Company and set out to build a line running from the center of the city to his Hyde Park. Shipe's franchise required him to have his line in operation under electric power by the end of February 1891. He beat the deadline, he later said, by just one hour and forty-four minutes. The *Cambridge Chronicle* reported that Barbour Stockwell's participation was critical to meeting the deadline. They prefabricated their part of the work, laid it out to insure all the parts fit in the firm's large yard and then took it apart and shipped it to Austin for installation. A similar project for Maine's Portland & Brunswick street railway was completed and delivered in sixty days.

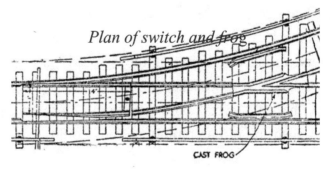

Plan of switch and frog

Making the straight sections of a railway is comparatively easy, but when the cars have to cross over to an alternate track they need the switch and frog assembly shown above. In the illustration, the Switch controls the Curved Closure Rail. If the rails are together as shown, the train wheels will move to the right in the direction of the curve. If the Switch pulls the Curved Closure Rail away, the train wheels will move along the Straight Main Rails. Only one of the ends of the Curved and Straight Closure Rails may be connected to the facing track at any time. To ensure that this is always the case the two Closure Rails are mechanically locked together. The Frog in the illustration ensures that the train wheels move smoothly in the selected direction.

Walworth Barbour's hometown of Saratoga had three different street railways in 1892. The *Kaydeross Railroad* connected water-powered textile mills along the river with the Delaware & Hudson Railroad. The *Schenectady Railway Company* had an extensive trolley system that connected Saratoga, Schenectady, Albany, and Troy. The *Hudson Valley Railway* started out as a horse-driven, narrow gauge road called the Glen Falls, Sandy Hill and Fort Edward St. R.R. Co. The Hudson Valley Railway served the more engaging spots of the region, and during the racing season at Saratoga it ran a special racetrack car from Troy to the racetrack at Saratoga in one hour and returned after the races without extra fare. During the season, this was one of the most popular cars on the road.

Persons could lunch in Troy after spending the morning in their office. After a delightful ride they could reach the racetrack in time for the afternoon sport, and then return in time for dinner. If a passenger preferred less sport, they could take the trolley to the famous Geyser Spring or the Florida Ostrich Farm that offered a correct representation of the original Florida farm that so many Northern people visited every year. In 1891, the Glen Falls, Sandy Hills and Fort Edwards lines began an extension and on April 10, 1892, a large order of frogs, switches, and special track to convert the railway to electricity was shipped out from 205 Broadway, Cambridge.

Dozens of US patents for street railway equipment were issued during the Second Industrial Revolution. One awarded in 1890 to Philip R. Downing of Boston related to "That class of street railway switches in which the switch is operated from the vehicle traveling upon the railway." With Downing's invention, if the driver wished to divert the train to a sidetrack, shortly before hitting the switch point he had to force down a mechanically pivoted arm that operated the switch, and the train wheels were shunted into the sidetracks. Within a year, Walter J. Bell in Los Angeles received a patent for a more advanced invention that allowed the motorman to switch a car onto a side rail without alighting from or stopping the vehicle by simply pressing an electric button. With Bell's invention, the switch was automatically reset to its former position.

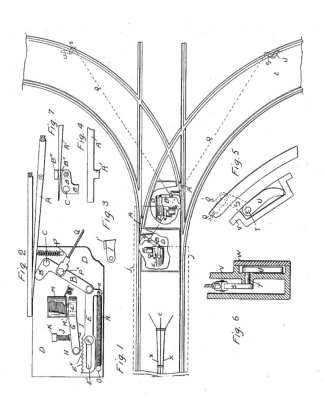

Walter Bell Switch

14: Printing

Cambridge as the seat of Harvard University must be considered to a certain extent as the educational center of America. What more natural, then, than that Cambridge should be the home of that art on which education most depends, the art preservative of all arts, the art and mystery of printing? As the home of such establishments as the Riverside Press, the University Press and the Atheneum Press, this city certainly enjoys a position of eminence in the printing and publishing trade that is unequaled by any city of its size in the country and that might well be envied by communities of much larger population.

This statement from the July 27, 1907, issue of the *Cambridge Chronicle* suggests another side to the city and its place in the Second Industrial Revolution. Although some of the major printers were not located right in Kendall Square, their adjacent locations and need for process machinery had to have ties to the machine tool makers. Innovations in the printing process were adding to the area's intense manufacturing activity. Some were made during the first half of the 19th century, when there were major changes in the machines used to make multiple prints. In 1824, Daniel Treadwell of Boston added gears and power to a wood-framed flat plate press making the operation four times faster. Eight years later New Yorker Richard Hoe introduced a cylinder press and in 1844 he invented the rotary press that could print up to 8,000 copies per hour on paper passed between two rollers. It was a time when ideas led to more ideas for machine tool makers on the East Coast. By 1865, William Bullock was inventing a press fed from a continuous roll of paper, boosting production to 12,000 pages per hour.

William Bullock Press

The time-consuming task of typesetting was shortened radically in 1880 with the advent of New Yorker Joseph's Thorne's Simplex/Unitype Type Setting Machine. It let you set type from a keyboard. It automated the tedious task of reorganizing type for re-use, and it provided the operator with the ability to enter entire words simultaneously. A happy user was quoted in the Mattoon, Illinois, Journal: "And the man who would attempt to remove the Simplex Type Setter from the journal office, were we unable to get another, would be shot on the spot, instanter."

The Thorne Simplex Machine

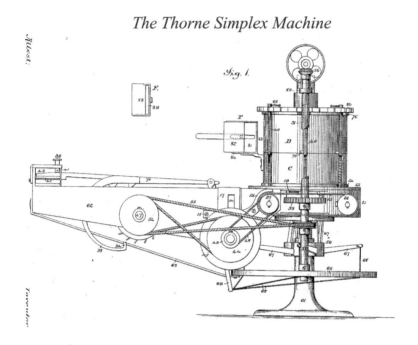

The Thorne machine was a commercial success, with almost 2,000 units sold over three decades. It was replaced over time by the much noisier Monotype or Linotype machine that was patented in 1886. Now, an operator could type on a keyboard and produce a perforated tape that in turn was decoded by a machine that cast type from hot metal. As opposed to the Thorne, which reused type, a Linotype machine melted the type after the press run.

In 1907, the Atheneum Press was located on First

Street, near Main in a four-story brick building, whose 200,000 square feet made it one of the largest manufacturing plants in Cambridge. The 500 employees of Atheneum Press published books for Ginn & Co, using electrotype printing, that could be done on lighter stock and the result was much more durable than versions printed with cast type. Electrotyping produced "an exact facsimile of any object having an irregular surface, whether it be an engraved steel or copper-plate, a wood-cut, or a form of set-up type, to be used for printing." The process was complicated and required skilled operators; but its accuracy was important in printing tomes like *Frye's Geographies*, which was turned out on large presses that could print a sheet forty-six by sixty inches Mattoon, Illinois, Journal: "And the man who would attempt to remove the Simplex Type Setter declared that "Teachers will find Frye's Geography clear, correct, scientific, comprehensive, and thoroughly up to date."

The Riverside Press started on Main Street but moved to Cambridgeport in 1864 and by 1910 employed more than 800 men, women, and boys. Henry O. Houghton and George Mifflin founded the firm, and in 1880 they merged with Ticknor and Fields, to combine the literary works of writers with the expertise of a publisher into a readers' conglomerate. Ticknor and Fields owned the Old Corner Book Store, the *Atlantic Monthly* and the *North American Review*. Ticknor and Fields also had an impressive list of authors that used the Old Corner Book Store as a place to meet: Horatio Alger, Lydia Maria Child, Charles Dickens, Ralph Waldo Emerson, Nathaniel Hawthorne, Oliver Wendell Holmes, Henry Wadsworth Longfellow, James Russell Lowell, Harriet Beecher Stowe, Alfred Tennyson, Henry David Thoreau, **Mark Twain, and** John Greenleaf Whittier. The new partnership kept the name of Houghton Mifflin and Company. In 1910, they had over eight hundred employees that divided their time working in either the paper warehouse, the press building with its sixty presses which processed up to 3,000 tons of paper each year, the bindery that could turn out 15,000 books per day, or the shipping and storage building that had three quarters of a million new books on hand at any time including a large number of Webster's International Dictionary that they printed for G.A.C. Merriam Co.

A year before the Riverside Press was founded, John L. Hammett, schoolteacher, author, salesman, started a new store in Rhode Island to sell school supplies. Two years later, in 1865, he moved the shop north to Boston, bringing with him his invention for a "slating paint," which prolonged the life of school slateboards. John also brought with him another item, which he conceived in the classroom after dropping the cloth that he and all his fellow teachers had been traditionally using to wipe away the day's lesson. Frustrated, John looked around for another piece of cloth and spied a carpet remnant, which he substituted for the cloth and immediately realized it was a far superior board wiper. After nailing carpeting to wood blocks, he included the new item in his growing sales catalogue, *School Supplies*. In 1915, John moved to Cambridge and built a new brick facility at 264 Main Street. From the new facility, they provided art craft materials, kindergarten blocks, pencils and paper of course, punchers, scissors, thumb tacks, blackboards, and chalk. A 1923 *Cambridge Tribune* article tells how, "Six miles of blackboard a yard wide is manufactured at their plant yearly," and "Enough paper has been manufactured there to go eight times around the world." Their 1930 catalogue of 150 pages had Illustrations showing thousands of school-related products, hundreds of them illustrated with engravings.

John Hammett built his Cambridge facility near the true center of Kendall Square. In recent years it has been the home of the MIT Press. Two years after Hammett built his, the taller Kendall Square Building was constructed on the east side of Hammett's and then the Suffolk Engraving and Printing Co. erected a loft building on the west side. All of these buildings were purchased by MIT, and, described by the historical society as the "Heart of Kendall Square," they have been preserved as one of the few remaining evidences of the industry that dominated Kendall Square during the Second Industrial Revolution.

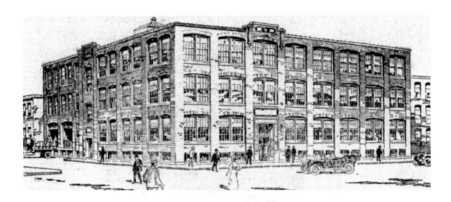

Architect's Rendering Hammett Building from Cambridge Chronicle 1913

The Hammett Company, Atheneum Press and Riverside Press were relative newcomers to Cambridge, when compared to the University Press that could trace its roots to the Daye Press that printed its first piece in 1638. Stephen Daye became the first printer in the United States by default, after a clergyman named Joseph Glover, who had planned to spread the word of God throughout the new colonies with his printing press, died before his ship reached Boston. Daye and three pressmen had accompanied Glover on the voyage, and Glover's widow, who inherited the press, put them all to work. The press was set up in the home of Harvard's first president, Henry Dunster, who promptly "married the press and took the woman with it." The first piece of work printed on the new press was a half-sheet pledging allegiance to the Commonwealth titled *Freeman's Oath*. It was followed by an *Almanack made for New England by Mr. Peirce, Marine.* The Day Press printed *The Whole Booke of Psalmes* in 1640, making it the first book printed in the United States. The press was taken over by son Matthew Daye after his father died in 1668, and by Samuel Green in 1649 after Matthew died. It changed various hands during a nearly print-stagnant 18th century until incorporated in 1850 as the University Press, owned by Welch, Bigelow & Co. In 1879, Welch, Bigelow & Co. failed and the business was purchased by John Wilson to create The University Press- John Wilson & Son.

15. Music and Money

Amongst the manufacturing activity and noises that predominated Kendall Square at the turn of the century were machines that make music. In 1905 Kendall Square was the home of two major manufacturers of pianos and organs, with a third located close by on Albany Street. Pianos were one of the few sources of music at the turn of the century, and over a thousand piano patents were issued in the United States and Europe during the 19th century, a half dozen of them to inventors in Cambridge like George Lutz, who received his for improvements in the sounding board. Cambridge inventors John McTammany, Jr. and Alfred William Nunn turned a piano into a machine when they received their patents for "player" pianos.

Cambridge was a logical place to manufacture pianos because the two materials needed to produce a quality sound were wood and cast iron.

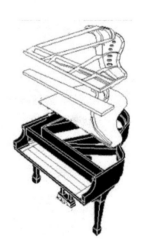

Given it's easy access to rails and waterfront, Kendall Square could easily import woods from all over the world. Hard maple and yellow birch came from northern New England and Canada, black walnut from the Ohio Valley, and mahogany from South America. It took skilled cabinetmakers to work the wood and skilled iron founders to cast the iron "plate" or iron frame that sits on top of the soundboard. Kendall Square had the men and women with the necessary experience to make and assemble the 2,500 odd parts. The plate on top of the soundboard had to accept the up to twenty tons of pressure from the tightened strings, and Alpheus Babcock from Boston set the industry standard for those iron frames when he received the first patent in 1825.

The new technologies of the Industrial Revolution provided piano manufacturers with the materials needed to produce a working cast iron plate, and improved steel production allowed them to use heavier gauge strings to create a richer sound. In 1859 the Steinway piano company invented a cross stringing method that allowed the strings to spread out and vibrate over a larger area, thereby producing a more resonant sound. Piano manufacturing in Cambridge started in 1865 with B. E. Colley & Company, a small-scale builder of square grand pianos and melodeons. Located in Cambridgeport, Colley received a number of patents, the last being listed in 1879; but he apparently ceased business in the 1880's. Ivers & Pond Piano

Company moved to Cambridge from Dedham in 1885. The factory was located at Main and Albany Streets in a six-story building whose increased height became easy to service because of the mid-century invention of the Otis elevator.

A piano was a major purchase for any family or institution; but Ivers & Pond were able to sell 3,000 finished pianofortes each year, using modest advertising like this in their 1895 catalogue:

> There is no magic in piano making. It is an experimental art, not an exact science, nor a secret process. Whatever one manufacturer may do is open to the world to examine and criticize, to experiment upon and improve; and the experience and judgment which direct wide experimenting are the qualities which tell. It so happens that we possess those qualities…We do not make a *perfect* piano; we know enough to know it, and we know enough to say it…We have capital enough to buy for cash and to sell on time; business men will understand the significance of this.

The house of Mason & Hamlin, founded in Boston in 1854, was relocated at the turn of the century across from Lever Brothers at 162 Broadway, Cambridge. They had a five-story brick building with 125,000 square feet of floor area. Their innovations that included their patented "tension resonator" won them the highest possible awards at the Paris World Exposition in 1867. Advertising in their 1906 catalogue was less self-effacing than Ivers & Pond's.

Reiteration of superlatives concerning the tone of the Mason & Hamlin Piano can convey no idea to the discriminating reader. The one test to be applied to a musical instrument is the hearing of it: no other proof can be as convincing. Tone quality in any musical instrument cannot be discovered without a hearing, and it cannot be described.

Mason & Hamlin also made organs, but not to the extent produced by Hutchings-Votey Organ Company located in 1904 on Albany Street, after a fire burned down their buildings in Boston. Two of their church organs were placed in Trinity Church, Boston, and others could be found in nearby Symphony Hall, the New England Conservatory of Music, Yale and Brown Universities, Vassar and Wellesley Colleges. The 27 July, 1907 *Cambridge Chronicle* claimed "This company stands preeminent among the organ building firms of this country, unexcelled, if indeed, it is equaled by any." George S. Hutchings, the founder and president, had done more to advance the art of church organ building than any other engaged in this line in the country. In 1903, Yale awarded him an M.A. in recognition of his genius in advancing the art of church organ design and construction.

There's no question that the dozens of manufacturing firms around Kendall Square at the turn of the 19th century provided innovation, manufacturing advances and vitality to the entire City of Cambridge. Many of these were start-ups, founded by young men without money of their own who had to borrow to succeed. The conglomerate corporate banks of today would smile at the fact that in 1900 Cambridge there were five national banks, four savings banks, and a trust company serving a city of less than 100,000; but banking was done differently in those days. In most cases, a few substantial men capitalized the banks, and these were the men you went to, to ask for a loan. The direct connection between the manufacturer and the money made it possible for inventors to conceive and make the production of sometimes risky ideas possible. Business transactions were done in cash, and that cash needed a safe place for storage. Each bank touted the impenetrability of their safe deposit vault and their proximity to their customers. To express both the stature and the security of where you placed your money, the Harvard Trust Company and the Cambridgeport Savings Bank constructed marble banking structures. Their imposing facades were also designed to encourage deposits from "industrious mechanics, widows, and orphans." If machines were the jewels of Kendall Square, the banks knew where they could be safely and profitably stored.

Cambridgeport Savings Bank

16. Packaging and Marketing

The products being produced in East Cambridge needed some form of packaging after they left the factory. In early days, hand packaging was typically employed to box or bag bulk items; but as machines were developed to produce goods for individual consumption, equivalent machinery was required for, and became much more important for, wrapping produce like candy and boxing the biscuits. Because most available wrapping materials were expensive, their use was limited to packaging luxury goods like watches and jewelry; but after WW I, they began shipping many consumer products in containers of molded glass, cardboard boxes, metal "tin" cans, and cellophane. Finally, items could be displayed on a store shelf and carried home without the need for handling and wrapping by a clerk, and the containers they were wrapped in had surfaces that could also become ideal locations for brand names, adding identity to utility.

All they needed were the means to persuade customers to buy things instead of making them at home and then to convince them to buy their particular brand rather than a competitor's. Happily it was a time when more Americans were becoming knowledgeable readers, especially those able to read the words on product packaging. With the increase in free public schooling, by

1880 the illiteracy rate had dropped to 17%. As the average American's ability to read increased, manufacturers found that advertising their wares not only increased sales, it also provided a way to install a desire to buy and possess. Subliminally, the new advertisements encouraged Americans to become fashionable and acquire goods that showed you were "worth something." Echoing Victorian trends in England, everyone here could rise up in class just by cluttering up their homes with symbols of mass-production. If advertising in newspapers, magazines and direct mail catalogues was to be really successful, however, manufacturers needed to brand their product with a distinctive name. This in turn meant that brand names needed to be protected, so the United States government created the first federal trademark law. Showing how important brand advertising had become, in 1899, out of fifteen trademarks recorded and protected by the law, six belonged to Lever Brother's for their laundry and toilet soaps.

Packaging a candy bar or cake of soap was fairly easy, if you had a machine that could wrap up the products in the square or rectangular shapes that storekeepers had developed over the years. Richard Berger from Brooklyn invented just such a machine and patented it in 1900, "for automatically wrapping articles, such as chocolate, caramels, gum, soap and other articles of such a size, as to make it desirable to use automatic means for rapidly and securely enclosing them in their wrap.... . A plurality of wrappers are preferably used, commonly two, such as wax paper for the inner wrapper, and metal foil for the outer wrapper. The wax paper protects the articles from contact with the foil." He further developed the idea into a more complex machine in 1908.

Berger Machines 1900 & 1908

Doing the same for eggs was far more difficult, because of the egg's shape and fragility. To keep a single egg stationary, it needed to be supported in at least three places. The first man to replace the homespun basket as an egg-carrying device was Thomas Bethell in Liverpool, England. His Raylite Egg Box consisted of frames made with interlocking strips of cardboard; but the first real egg carton was invented in 1911 by a Canadian newspaper editor named Joseph Coyle, who used it to solve a dispute between a hotel owner and local farmer as to who broke the eggs, or when and how were they broken before the chef started to use them? Coyle's solution was a start but his carton still didn't provide a tight, three-point suspension system for each egg.

Although, even today, we still have to check the carton for damages before checking out at a supermarket, the answer to safely packaging eggs would come from a material that could be molded almost to the given item's shape. The idea for that came from Martin L. Keyes, who was working in a wood veneer plant in New York, where he saw workers eating their lunches off of small sheets of hardwood veneer. Adding that to his mother's desire to improve on the pressed wood pie plates that she was using, Keyes was prompted to form wood pulp into a mold. To do that he needed a machine that would mash the pulp, mold it, and finally dry it. After successive attempts to design such a machine, he finally perfected a design for one that was good enough for him to construct a model. He reportedly took his drawings to a "friend who owned an iron works" and the first machine was constructed at 373 Broadway in Cambridge, not that far from Kendall Square. Keyes' invention used a two-part mold with a space in between where the product was formed. Simply put, it was a perforated mold immersed into pulp slurry. When suction was applied to the mold, it caused a layer of slurry to stick to the mold.)

Martin L. Keyes Molding Machine

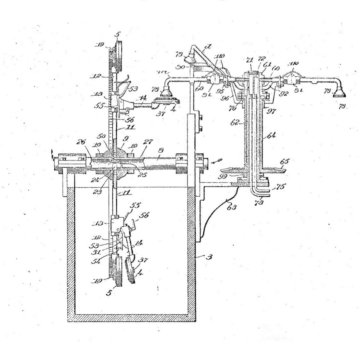

Keyes attempted to patent his machine, but was told that the process was already patented. Realizing that his ideas had been stolen, he produced his lengthy diaries that described step-by-step how he'd created his Apparatus for Making Pulp Articles; and he finally acquired its basic patent. The Keyes Fiber Company that emerged from this was incorporated in Shawmut, Maine. It produced molded pulp products and eventually had major plants in Indiana, California, Washington, and Louisiana. Keyes' patent didn't limit others from using wood pulp to mold a form, and in 1921, Morris Koppelman of Brooklyn, New York, invented a product that "relates to the packing of eggs and similar articles which are fragile or likely to be injured by jarring or contact with one another, and it is in the nature of an improvement on the invention disclosed in a co-pending application." His application showed a box with cups at top and bottom to hold an egg in place, which looked good in a drawing, but might be impractical if any of the eggs were out of line when the top cover with its cups was closed down. A later patent application in 1927 showed tops and bottoms shaped "preferably by the pulp sucking or felting process in which floating fibers are drawn by suction against a screen." His Holed Tight Packaging Corporation continued applying for patents and trademarks on its name into the 1930's.

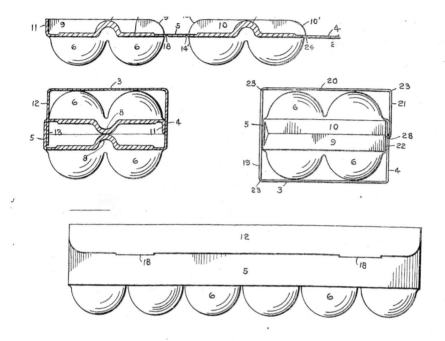

After Koppleman, there were multiple patent applications related to cartons for eggs or similarly fragile items like light bulbs. One awarded to Diamond International was more "particularly directed to improvements in the cover of a container and the manner in which the cover cooperates with a cellular tray." On Commercial Street in East Cambridge, MIT graduate Grenville B. Gerrish began working on an invention that would accelerate the pulp fiber drying process, which apparently was a problem with the intricate shapes of the evolving egg carton. In 1954 he applied for a patent for a machine "utilizing a multiplicity of jets of high velocity of drying air or gas so arranged in pattern and numbers with reference to the particular articles to be dried, that substantially uniform drying of the entire article is produced even though the character of the article may differ markedly in different portions." Further, "Each cup being designed to receive an egg therein, and a cover which may be closed down over the eggs contained in the pockets and be sealed in closed position if this should be desired…" A concern for the cover was important; because eggs, unlike many other foodstuffs, come to the grocery shelf with a brand name and advertisements for its quality directly printed on the cover. You can't boil, fry, or scramble your breakfast without seeing its source every morning.

Grenville Gerrish Egg Carton Making Machine

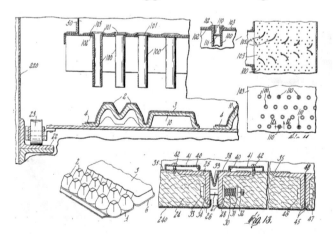

Gerrish received other patents for his Wolverine Manufacturing Company that, like those of his predecessors, became important for packaging more than eggs. As the world developed a call for more environmentally sound shipping materials and was producing a plethora of different shaped consumer goods that complicated their packaging, molded pulp, with its unique cushioning characteristics, answered both challenges. Expanded polystyrene foam couldn't do that. An increasing use of the Internet for consumer shopping directly from the producer also developed a need for packaging items that used to be carried home in a paper bag. Amazon, Wal-Mart, Cosco, and others began servicing millions through the Internet that in turn would receive their purchases in packages. In 1940, Stanley Price and Edward Sloan of Lucent Technologies received the first patent for the use of molded fiber as a packaging material for those consumer goods, in this case telephone handsets. The Price and Sloan references included the work of Martin Keyes. Over a century has passed since Keyes's invention; and molded pulp, improved over those years, is still a favorite form of packaging.

In an age before television, Marketing or promoting the product depended not just on the branding and packaging, but upon the product itself. One of the first at the turn of the century to make a product that in a way was self-marketing was a man named King Gillette. Gillette and all other men who shaved did so with a wedge-shaped, heavy metal blade that had been forged and had to be kept sharpened by stropping it on a leather belt. Traveling salesmen called them cut-throat razors after trying to use them on a bouncing train. As an alternative, Gillette had an idea in 1895 to fabricate a razor that could be firmly held in the hand and had a disposable blade. When metallurgists told him that manufacturing his disposable blade was unfeasible, he sought out help from MIT graduate William Nickerson. After six years of experimentation, the pair produced a machine that could produce the disposable blade and patented it in 1901. Sales for the Gillette Safety Razor Company grew rapidly, aided by the U.S. Government that issued about 3.5 million razors and 32 million blades to World War I soldiers. This was enough to turn the rest of the nation into safety razor users. In all of this, Gillette kept selling his patented razor at or below cost. He made his fortune selling the profitable disposable blades.

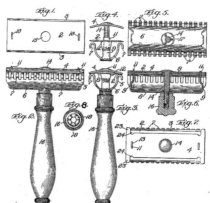

17. Human Engineering

The Second Industrial Revolution produced machines that would repeatedly duplicate the exact same part, making them interchangeable and appropriate for mass production. The word "handmade" became merely a label for unique gifts or the product of a hobby shop. Invention led to invention and each new machine tool meant that more humans could be freed from physical drudgery. At first, the power to operate these tools came from steam turbines that rotated multiple overhead shafts on each factory floor. Belts from the overhead shafts dropped down to the working surface and the revolving shaft of each machine. Gathering together as many machines as possible, getting their power from a central boiler plant, increased overall efficiencies; but it also concentrated the human operators in multi-storied buildings, making them both a captive workforce and a cohesive group that could act in its own interest.

Work in a Kendall Square factory could become dangerous. In 1912, 35.7 percent of all of the work-related accidents in Massachusetts were caused by machinery versus 3.9 percent with hand tools. The estimated loss in terms of work hours exceeded 2,000,000. Most workers understood the risks, as long as the rewards were worth it; but the new concept of payment for work by the hour meant that the employer could control the hourly wage, often at will. It was an era ripe for strikes, particularly in the sweat-intensive foundries where the melting point for gray cast iron was above 2000 degrees Fahrenheit. In the first half of the 19th century, employers easily countered strikes among iron s by importing immigrants to do the work. Some s responded by setting up their own small foundries. Others formed friendly and benevolent societies in an attempt to negotiate better wages and working conditions. By 1850, there were few Eastern cities that didn't have such an association, but attempts to organize them nationally failed until 1864 when the iron molders formed the Iron Workers' International Union at a convention in Buffalo, New York and elected William H. Sylvis as president. Now a local union could get the support of neighboring organizations during a strike. At first a company like Barbour Stockwell seemed to be a step ahead of the unions. In 1893, they lowered the foundry working hours from ten to nine a day, without reducing the day's pay. As a result, Barbour Stockwell reported in November, 1894 that business was much larger than the previous year. An action that benefited both parties was short lived. On September 20, 1895, the officers of Iron Workers' Union 106 ordered their membership to strike for a minimum wage of $2.50 per day. The 300 ironworkers employed at Barbour-Stockwell walked out along with workers from foundries in East Boston and Roxbury.

Laborer antagonism was hard to accept for those company owners who had worked their way up from the bottom. Those with a long family history as industrialists, saw the strikes as an inevitable part of doing business. The strikers were organized but so were the employers. Foundry owners, for instance, had the New England Foundrymen's Association. Within the organization, agreements about acceptable wages, even if not explicit, could be made amongst members. The system worked both ways. In 1897, one company locked out 34 members of Union 106 for refusing to sign an agreement that the union said required a longer working day without extra wages and abrogated an agreement made with the Foundrymen's Association in 1895. It was reported that "not one of the thirty-four who went out returned to work, and furthermore the company asserted that their places had been filled. The company said that no more men were wanted and that work was progressing satisfactorily."

To operate the new clusters of machinery, many laborers came from the farms; but the new factories around Kendall Square could also call upon the Irish immigrants who made up twenty-two percent of the population of East Cambridge. These unfortunates had to leave their homeland after a unique strain of potato blight imported from the mid-Americas, that they now call HERB- 1, created a mass famine. Around the turn of the twentieth century, immigrants from Italy, Poland, and Portugal arrived in the city, also settling in Cambridgeport and East Cambridge. The area's increasing industrialization required an expanded workforce and many of these immigrants left their first labor-intensive jobs in the clay pits and brickyards of North Cambridge to work in the Kendall Square mills. Kendall Square was booming as a center of trade. In fact, the Panic 0f 1873-78, which at the time was considered the worst economic depression in American history, hardly hit the City of Cambridge.

For some of the newcomers, the steps up from clay pit to factory led even further. Slowly, the Irish population of East Cambridge entered the political scene, as the city fought over different forms of government to replace what had been a Common Council of respected citizens. Discussions of the resulting "political machine" and corrupt government prompted debate on changes to its political system in the early twentieth century. In 1911, voters shot down a proposal that included removing party names from local ballots, the right of referendum, initiative, and recall, and a new structure of voting. In 1915, Cambridge opted for Plan B of several offered by the state, which restructured city administration with the hope of making it more transparent and representative. For the next fifteen years, people debated less about the structure of government, but more about the underlying issues of rising property taxes, more corruption, proportional representation, and tenement housing. Other issues became the platforms for a plethora of newly oriented groups, such as the Cambridge Housing Association and the League of Women Voters.

The Second Industrial Revolution opened avenues for advancement for millions of Americans. It may have introduced new demands on human minds and bodies, but these were mostly offset by inventions that improved lifestyles. One was the introduction of electricity as a power source around the turn of the century that provided Indianan Fred W. Wolf an opportunity to patent a refrigerator for home use in 1913. This meant fresh foods could be kept so for longer periods and in turn improve the health of a household. Electricity also provided the world with the X-ray, discovered by German scientist Conrad Röntgen in 1895. While experimenting with electrical currents through glass cathode-ray tubes, he discovered that a piece of barium platinocyanide glowed even though the tube was encased in thick black cardboard and was across the room. In 1903 Willem Einthoven, a Dutch doctor and physiologist, invented the first practical electrocardiogram (ECG or EKG). These discoveries are basic to our good health today; but were hardly available to many of the poor men, women, and children employed in the new candy, biscuit, and machine-tool factories that were clustering in East Cambridge. Although manufacturers were creating generous returns to the stockholders and the ten financial institutions in Cambridge were thriving, the area itself was neglected, as *Cambridge Considered* described conditions in their *A Very Brief History of Cambridge, 1900-2000.*

The growth was not limited to major industries. Cantabrigians bound books, made musical instruments, engines, industrial-scale boilers, and cars, laid railroad track, and built bridges. However, industrialization was a mixed blessing. For example, in the 1890's, East Cambridge typified a dirty modern city. Meatpacking and fertilizer were among the most offensive of the many industries that contributed to the odor and uncleanliness of the area.

Similar conditions existed in the residential areas of East Cambridge where rapid growth resulted in unsanitary conditions and the spread of disease was always there. In *The Paradox of Public Health in a Time of Crisis*, David Rosner listed the health issues.

In the absence of sewer systems, pure water, systematic street cleaning, pure or fresh food or milk, and decent methods for preserving or freezing meats, diphtheria and whooping cough, typhoid, typhus, and any number of fevers and influenzas became constant threats to babies and young children in the filthy urban trading centers of the nation...Along with crowding came a decided decline in the quality of life for many. In the nation's growing cities, it is estimated that there were as many as one horse for every 10 to 20 residents, and each horse deposited between 30 and 50 pounds of manure and two quarts of fresh urine a day on city streets.

As East Cambridge came up with new innovations and a resulting growth of manufacturing, the phenomena also produced the demise of some Kendall Square industries. The electric railway and the automobile eventually replaced the need for thousands of horses and the stables of E. R. Luke & Co. on Main Street closed down. Centralizing power and distributing electricity would eliminate the need for coal and wood deliveries and at the same time put David Proudfoot at 84 Bridge Street, and The Bay State Fuel Company at 157 Main Street that employed 175 men with 70 delivery teams, out of business. John E. Ryan at 15 River Street would find few markets for hay, grain, and mineral salt. Hugh Stewart & Co. at 414 Main Street was one of the best known wagon and carriage builders in New England. Stephen J. Moran on Main Street was another. Henderson Brothers on Massachusetts Avenue manufactured carriages in a five-story building that also housed a 2500 horse-drawn vehicle exhibition hall considered one of the sights of Boston. John J. Fritz at 370 River Street painted carriages. L. C. Chase & Co. on Albany Street specialized in manufacturing Horse Clothing with a staff of 200. F.A. Tippet on Sidney Street sold Pratt's Astral oil and Phoenix illuminating oil. Every one of them would disappear as a result of the Second Industrial Revolution.

If you lived near Harvard Square at the turn of the

century, educating Harvard students would have seemed to be the prime industry of Cambridge. How could the oldest institution for learning in the United States be considered otherwise? Harvard already had its medical and law schools and it created a business school in 1908. At that time, the Charles River lapped land just south of Main Street, leaving a ragged shoreline that was used as a dumping ground for things like the discarded sand molds from the area's foundries. In 1911, they started the progressive filling of 46 acres for a cost of one million dollars to create usable land and a new parkway along the Charles River called Memorial Drive. In 1916, Harvard had to welcome a collegiate companion down river when the Massachusetts Institute of Technology moved over from Boston to occupy some of the filled land. It's key subway stop: Kendall Square. Harvard wasn't all that happy about its new neighbor, which its President, Charles William Eliot, had tried to buy three times. Now that it was a fete accompli, its new president, A. Lawrence Lowell, worried that MIT would add to the city's tax burden. Since its inception, Harvard had not paid taxes on its ever-growing amounts of land, and Lowell feared that MIT would be the tipping point at which the city started asking for taxes from private institutions of higher learning. Cambridge never did start asking Harvard or MIT to pay taxes, because the schools decided to pay the city an annual lump sum instead.

Epilogue

It was the 1930's. For the first time since the 17th century, the manufacturing firms and the population of Cambridge began to shrink. The entire world was in a depression; but Cambridge's residential problems went deeper and were endemic. The few who could afford to moved away to the growing, primarily commuter suburbs like Winchester, Belmont, or Newton; the rest moved out as their workplaces disappeared. The candy business was a significant hold-out. In 1910 there were 16 candy manufacturers listed in the city, by 1920 there were 30, and by 1930 there were more than 40. Firms like George Close and Daggett Chocolates merged with Necco, so much of their production remained in Cambridge until Necco itself moved out in 2003. James O. Welch's production of *Sugar Daddies* and *Junior Mints* and Fox Cross's *Charlestown Chew* moved over to Tootsie Roll Industries, but most of the Welch candies were still produced in the original Cambridge plants. It took many years for Main Street's title as "Confectioner's Row" to be diminished. The manufacturers of Biscuits and Crackers, however, didn't stay as long in Cambridge. The Kennedy Biscuit Company, originator of the *Fig Newton,* became part of Nabisco; and, although the brand name and their famous *Oreo* cookies still dominate supermarket shelves, the company itself was merged, traded, leveraged, and agglomerated a number of times and the production facilities were moved to Chicago. Just as it once left Cambridge, half of that production was moved to Mexico and lower labor costs.

By 1929, Lever Brothers in Kendall Square was the third-largest soap manufacturer in the country, employing approximately 1,000 workers in Cambridge and 1,400 workers total across the United States. They occupied four city blocks with the main buildings fronting on Broadway near Kendall Square. Throughout the 1930's and 1940's, the company continued to experience steady growth in sales. While its overseas parent company was reorganized and merged into the new company of Unilever, the American Lever Brothers Company kept its name. The American branch of the company acquired Pepsodent and one of their key persons named Charles Luckman. Although educated as an architect, Luckman had taken a job as a draftsman with Pepsodent during the Depression and rose up through the ranks to become its president. During World War II, Luckman moved over to Lever Brothers and soon became its president. One of his first projects was to move all of the executives off the top floor of the Lever Brothers office building that had been built along Memorial Drive and occupy the mammoth space with a single large president's desk located at the opposite end of the floor from the elevators. This bold move seemed to many like the kind of space Albert Speer was designing for Nazi Germany.

Luckman's next radical step was to commission architects Skidmore Owings & Merrill to design a new glass tower in New York, and Lever house became the new company headquarters and the first skyscraper of its kind in Manhattan. It's said that Luckman's demise came in 1946, after he apparently tried to corner the market on the tallow needed to make conventional soap just when Proctor & Gamble introduced *Tide*. The revolutionary synthetic cleaning detergent that didn't need the tallow would soon make the Cambridge plant buildings along Broadway obsolete.

In Cambridge, street railway systems progressed from horse-drawn to electric powered streetcars and were the best possible mode of transportation around the turn of the 19th century. Nearly every city and town in America of more than 2,500 people had its own electric rail system. Almost ninety percent of all trips were by electric rail. Street and interurban railways were a thriving and profitable industry with 44,000 miles of track, 300,000 employees, 15 billion annual passengers, and $1 billion in income. Although On May 26, 1927, Henry Ford watched the 15 millionth Model T Ford roll off the assembly line at his factory in Highland Park, Michigan, less than twenty percent of Americans owned an automobile. Nevertheless, the auto market appeared to be saturated to Alfred P. Sloan, Jr. of General Motors, so he developed a special unit within the corporation charged with the task of replacing

American street railways with cars, trucks, and buses. They acquired a controlling share of the Yellow Coach Manufacturing Company. Similarly, John D. Hertz formed the Omnibus Corporation that then purchased New York's Fifth Avenue Coach Company.

By 1930 most streetcar systems were aging, losing money, and service to the public was suffering. The Great Depression only increased their problems. Yellow Coach management tried to persuade transit companies to replace their streetcars with buses. GM formed a new subsidiary, United Cities Motor Transport, to finance the conversion of streetcar systems to buses in small cities. For decades, GM was the nation's largest shipper of freight over railroads, which in turn controlled some of America's most extensive railways. By wielding freight traffic as a club, GM persuaded railroads to abandon their electric rail subsidiaries. Making Frogs and Sprockets became a diminishing business for firms in Kendall Square.

A company like Barbour Stockwell worked through the Depression years making machine tools for firms like Lever Brothers, producing Reliance Tachometers to check revolutions or traveled miles on a moving wheel, devising machines to wrap and package underwear, and creating freezing systems for Clarence Birdseye's quick frozen foods. The iron foundry produced Sewer grates for storm water systems, one of which ended up as an item of history. A *Smithsonian* article written by Richard & Joyce

Wolkomir talks about a Harvard professor named John Robert Stilgoe, who they labeled a *scholar of the ordinary*. As their story developed, Stilgoe was looking for historic artifacts when he noticed an iron disk embedded in the pavement. It was the Barbour Stockwell name that interested him, because it came from one of the old Cambridge foundries.

Photograph of Sewer Grate by Melikamp

To Stilgoe, such a humble artifact as a manhole cover or fire hydrant was a true portal of the past. Born in 1949, Stilgoe is the Robert and Lois Orchard Professor in the History of Landscape at the Visual and Environmental Studies Department of <u>Harvard University</u>. Here is how Stilgoe looks to the world around him:

> Education ought to work outdoors, in the rain and the sleet, in the knife-like heat of a summertime Nebraska wheat field, along a half-abandoned railroad track on a dark autumn afternoon, on the North Atlantic in

winter. All that I do is urge my students and my readers to look around, to realize how wonderfully rich is the built environment, even if the environment is only a lifeboat close-hauled in a chiaroscuro sea."

By the 1950's the last Stockwell connected with that firm was a real estate broker by profession and the company briefly became a subsidiary of the Peter Gray Company before the buildings were demolished and the land was sold, awaiting the revival of the Kendall Square corridor. That revival, which was initiated in 1982 by MIT professor Philip Sharp and Wally Gilbert when they moved their new biotechnology company called Biogen into a vacant factory building on Binney Street, increased its boundaries as the Internet grew and the large hardware-intensive computing companies that needed equally large spaces were being replaced with small start-ups that required much less square footage. They found that kind of space for their desk-top computer operations in the Cambridge Innovation Center at One Broadway. Then, venture capitalists were looking for space to be near the start-ups they might be financing. The number of new arrivals again changed when Novartis took over the Necco Candy building in 2003 and added 2,000 new employees to the working population. They were followed by Pfizer, Amgen, AstraZeneca, and Baxter. The original move-in, Professor Sharp's Biogen, then moved out to the suburbs and soon moved back. By 2009, the Boston Consulting Group proclaimed Kendall

Square—an area roughly defined as everything within a 10-minute walk of the Kendall subway station—"the most innovative square mile on earth."

Six years later, the *MIT News Office* announced a new plan for Kendall Square on September 9, 2015 in *MIT presents its Kendall Square Initiative to Cambridge Planning Board:*

> Since 2010, MIT has been working with the broader community to advance a proposal to bring new vibrancy and diversity to Kendall Square... MIT is now poised to deliver a dynamic blend of uses in this area...and will advance the pace of life-changing science by attracting innovative companies and strengthening vital collaborations within the Kendall Square ecosystem.

The article describes what the planning board approved in May, 2016 as a "Kendall Square innovation district" consisting of six new buildings. These will provide a mix of affordable and market-rate housing, new student residential units, research and development buildings, and more than 100,000 square feet of retail space. Within a year, another new opportunity for growth appeared with the lots that had held buildings of the Peter Gray & Company and architect Benjamin Fox. They had been consolidated with others into a single property bounded by Broadway, Third Street, Binney Street, and the Mid-Block Connector known as the Volpe Center. The site had a varied past. In the mid-1960's it was a low-rise neighborhood with a lot of aging industrial buildings, when NASA announced plans to locate a new Electronic Research Center there on land next to MIT, which would employ 3,000 people. Square. Given the NASA intended move, the City of Cambridge leveled buildings, cleared land, and improved the roads on twenty-nine acres to be occupied by NASA. Encouraged by the initial support of President Kennedy, six of fourteen planned buildings had been constructed by 1969, when Richard Nixon, the newly-elected president, ordered the facility closed in a round of budget cuts. Although former Governor John Volpe was able to convince the government to use the six buildings to house the National Transportation Center, the rest of the site became a giant parking lot sometimes called *Nowhere Square.* Beyond its dreary visage, the now-vacated blocks left little to bolster the city's diminished tax base.

In January, 2017, MIT signed an agreement with the U.S. General Services Administration (GSA) with the intent of turning the federally owned Volpe property into a more vibrant mixed-use site that would benefit both MIT and the Cambridge community. According to the agreement, MIT agrees to construct a new federal building on the Volpe Center site. Following its construction, the Institute will receive ownership of the balance of the property, which it will then develop. At approximately 14 acres, the site now includes six buildings, open areas of landscaped land, and two parking lots that take up most of the land area. The Point that grew first to manufacture the products of inventors in the Second Industrial Revolution would rise again as a base, in the words of President L. Rafael Reif, "To help the people of MIT deliver their ideas to the world. Innovation is all about human collision, and the power of proximity of the labs and those who can apply the science. We're curating our front yard, if you will, to make that happen."

Bibliography

Beale, Joseph H. The history of local government in Cambridge. Abstract, January 26, 1932

"Brattleboro Water Cure" New Haven Courier. brattleborohistory.com/medicine/water-cure----hydropathic-house.html

Brown, Emil The Baker's Handbook, 1902 Andesite Press. August 11, 2015

Candyland: The Cambridge Historical Society

"Civil engineering," Proceedings of the American Society of Civil Engineers, Volume 40. 1914

Costs, Street Railway Review, 1891

Daggett and Young Families Candy Daggett Young, Gateway Press, 1982

Deacon Edward Kendall, Cambridge Tribune 9 January 1915

The Enrober, Savyjean & Co.

Famous as a Bookproducing City, Cambridge Chronicle, 12 January, 1901

Foundry Strike, Cambridge Chronicle Feb 13, 1897

Foundry Unions, International Molders' Journal, Nov, Dec 1911

Foss,Alden S. "Boston Woven Hose and Rubber Company: Eighty- Four Years in Cambridge." Cambridge Historical Society, Volume 40,   1964-1966

Fundamentals of Modern Manufacturing , Materials, Processes, and Systems. CTI Reviews. 2016

Garner, Nicole. "The Revolutionary Story Behind Mary Jane Candies." Mental Floss October 29, 2015. Mentalfloss.com"

Garrison, J. Ritchie. Hydropathy and the Lawrence water cure, Two Carpenters:Architecture and Building in Early New England, 1799-1859

Gilman, Arthur. The Cambridge of eighteen hundred and ninety-six: a picture of the city and its industries fifty years after its incorporation. Riverside Press 1896

Hershey's: Our Story. Hersheys.com. September 4, 2017

History of Cambridge, Massachusetts. 1630-1877:archive.org/details/historyofcambrid01paig

History of Middlesex County, Massachusetts 1880

History of the West End Street Railway: archive.org/details/historyofwestend

Industry in Cambridge: The Cambridge Historical Society

Innovation in Cambridge: The Cambridge Historical Society

The Iron Founder Supplement of 1893.

Iron Molders International Union, 1913

Ivers & Pond Catalogue 1895Klein, Maury. The Genesis of Industrial America, 1870-1920. Cambridge University Press September, 2007

Mason- Hamlin Catalogue 1906

Milk Chocolate History, What's Cooking Americas.net

MIT presents its Kendall Square Initiative to Cambridge Planning Board: MIT News Office, September 9, 2015

"McKinsey, James O. "Organization and Methods of the Walworth Manufacturing Company." Journal of Political Economy,vol. 30, no. 3, 1922

Murray, Albert N. The Story of Kendall Square. 1915. From old catalogue. Nabu Press. 2014

Nabisco. mondelezinternational.com June,18, 2017

NECCO History. Necco.com. August 31,2017

Obrien, Geoffrey. The Fall of the House of Walworth, A Tale of Madness and Murder in Gilded Age America. Holt. July 20,2010

Ollive, Thomas S."Some Reminiscences of a Lifetime Spent in the Baking Business." Bakers Review. April, 1916

The Origins and History of Candy. candyhistory.net December 12. 2017

The Past and Future of Kendall Square, Technology Review, August, 2015,

The Printing Industry, Cambridge Chronicle 6 May,1911

Progressive Young Cambridge Firm, Cambridge Chronicle, Mar 19,1892

Industrial Cambridge, Cambridge Tribune, July 27, 1907

Industrial and Building Edition, Cambridge Chronicle, Sept 9 1905

Industrial League Schedule. Cambridge Tribune, June 25, 1921

"James Fisk, Jr." Vermont Phoenix, May 22, 1858

Journal: Mattoon, Illinois

Journal of the Association of Engineering Societies, 1909

Kendall Boiler and Tank Co. kendallboiler.com/our-history July 11, 2017

Listings in Cambridge, Massachusetts, National Register of Historic Places

Luther Patent, Cambridge Chronicle November 1, 1894

Now a Pitiable Wreck, Cambridge Chronicle December 5, 1897 1897

Our Neighbors at Kendall Square, Cambridge Tribune in November, 1923.

Mokyr, Joel. The Second Industrial Revolution. 1870-1914
Abstract, Northwestern University

Moulders Union Strike, Boston Daily Globe, Sept 28 1895

Pamphlets Contain a Short Story of Cambridge, Cambridge
Tribune 15 July,1922

A Progressive, Young Cambridge Firm, Cambridge Tribune 19
March, 1892

Parks, Roger N. Roads in New England, 1790-1840. Report by
the Department of Research Old Sturbridge Village

Palmer, Foster M. "Horse Car, Trolley, And Subway."
Proceedings of the Cambridge Historical Society, 39 (1961-63.)

Printing In Cambridge Since 1800: Norman Hill White, January
1920

Rosner, David. "Spanish Flu or whatever it is…The Paradox of
Public Health in a Time of Crisis." Public Health Reports.
April, 2010

Restoration: Cantabile Piano Arts, Yonkers, NY,
cantabilepianoarts.com

Seaburg, Alan and Thomas Dahill, Carol Rose. Cambridge on
the Charles, The Anne Miniver Press. 2001

Snell, Bradford. The Street Car Conspiracy: How General
Motors Deliberately
Destroyed Public Transit. lovearth.net/
gmdeliberatelydestroyed.htm November 10, 2017

Some out in Cambridge, Cambridge Chronicle Mar 11, 1902

Speirs, Frederick W. The street railway system of Philadelphia;
its history and present condition, 1867-1905

Steam Engine: UXL Encyclopedia of Science 2002, The Gale
Group, Inc.

Stone, Orra L. The History of Massachusetts Industry. S.J. Clarke Publishing Co. 1930

The Street Railway Review of 1891. American Street Railway Association Street Railway Accountants' Association of America American Railway,Mechanical, and Electrical Association. Street Railway Review. 1891

The Strikers Rejoice, Cambridge Chronicle, May 5, 1892

Thompson, Zadok. History of Vermont 1842 Nabu Press. April 6, 2012

Timeline of historic inventions, Wickipedia

Trade Association Cambridge Tribune, 2 June, 1894

"Twentieth-Century Business Archives" Lehman Brothers Collection. library.hbs.edu/hc/lehman/papers.html

A Very Brief History of Cambridge, 1900-2000, Part I: The Turn of the Century   Through Plan E."cambridgeconsidered.blogspot.com/2011/07/very-brief-history-of-cambridge- 1900.html. March 20,2017

Wever, Renee and Diana Twede. The History of Molded Fiber Packaging; a 20th Century Pulp Story. Abstract. researchgate.net January 10, 2018

When candy was king. Newenglandhistoricalsociety.com

Watt, Alexander The Art of Soap-Making: CreateSpace Independent Publishing Platform   1901   (2017)

Wolkomir, Richard and Joyce Wolkomir. "Reading the Messages in Everyday Things" Smithsonian. April, 2000

By the Author:

The Book of Quinton
· *The 1677 massacre and forced march of captives from Hatfield and Deerfield, Mass. Twenty were captured and force marched from Deerfield to Canada. Seventeen returned to tell their story.*
· By Sherwood Stockwell & Quinton Stockwell
· 126 Pages, 2018

MY MOUNTAINS
· *Over a lifetime, many personal and professional moments happened near or because of mountains. This memoir ties one to the other.*
· By Sherwood Stockwell
· 264 Pages, 2018

The Perfect Berry!
· *It must taste good, be good for you, easy to come by, affordable. Blueberries are available 365 days a year. A determined young lady, a dedicated botanist, three neuroscientists, packaging experts, and world-wide marketers made it happen*
· By Sherwood Stockwell
· 40 Pages, 2018,

A Week in the Open
· *Five determined women declare their independence from Victorian norms in a tale set in California's Gold Country that was recorded 100 years ago by one of them, and only recently discovered.*
· By Ruth Crane, Sherwood Stockwell
· 48 Pages, 2018

CPSIA information can be obtained
at www.ICGtesting.com
Printed in the USA
BVHW041555151118
533214BV00020B/630/P

9 780464 862826